D1629778

Preparing
Young
Children
For
Math

Preparing Young Children For Math
A Book of Games

Claudia Zaslavsky

**Illustrations by
Sam Zaslavsky**

SCHOCKEN BOOKS • NEW YORK

First published by Schocken Books 1979

10 9 8 7 6 5 4 3 2 1   79 80 81 82

Library of Congress Cataloging in Publication Data

Zaslavsky, Claudia.
　Preparing young children for math.

　Bibliography: p.
　Includes index.
　1. Mathematics—Study and teaching (Primary)
2. Mathematical recreations.　I. Title.
QA135.5.Z37　　　　　　　372.7　　　　　79-12552

Manufactured in the United States of America

Dedicated to Tom and Alan,
from whom I learned about children.

Contents

Preface   ix

Introduction   xi

I. WHAT PARENTS CAN DO   1

II. HOW TO PLAY THE GAMES   9

III. EARLY GAMES   13

  Shape and Space
    Introduction
    Games
  Sorting and Comparing
    Introduction
    Games
  Number
    Introduction
    Games

IV. SHAPE AND SPACE GAMES   39

  Introduction
  Games

V. MEASUREMENT GAMES   61

Introduction
Games

VI. NUMBER GAMES   81

Introduction
Games

APPENDIX   119

A. The Metric System
B. Recommended Children's Books
C. Songs and Singing Games
D. Beautiful Junk
E. Commercial Materials
F. Board and Table Games
G. Adult Books and Resources
H. Resource Catalogs

Preface

This book is intended for all caregivers of young children. Its goal is to make "doing math" as natural an activity as talking.

Although chapter 1 is addressed primarily to parents, the games and guiding information offered in the following chapters are equally suitable for classroom and home use. Teachers of nursery schools, day care centers, Head Start and Follow Through programs, kindergartens, and early elementary grades will find that these activities fit comfortably into the normal school routine.

The games, arranged in three carefully graded sequences, are based on the most up-to-date research on how children learn. While providing many hours of fun and togetherness, such activities will be very effective in preparing children for the mathematics they will need in later years.

The games are designed for use with both girls and boys. Feminine and masculine pronouns are used in alternate sections of the book, but do not reflect the nature of the activity being described in any single passage.

It is a pleasure to acknowledge the help I received in writing this book. Grace Cohen, Herbert Ginsburg, Doris Hartman, Mary Ann Porcher, Anne Rubenstein, and Marion Walter criticized various parts of the manuscript. I owe thanks to the children who tried out many of the games, as well as to their very cooperative parents and grandparents—to Rasha Hamid, Sora Deetza Luchins, and to all three Lustig children, Jason, Karya, and Yanos, who proved that older sisters and brothers can be excellent teachers.

Introduction

Mathematics has become part of our lives to an ever greater degree. To understand the national budget or batting averages, complex computers or hand-held calculators, some knowledge of mathematics is required. Preparation for such nonmathematical careers as management, teaching, and social work includes courses in statistics and other branches of mathematics. Women and minorities in ever greater numbers are entering professional fields in which mathematical training is essential.

Educators are broadening the school curriculum to take into account the growing need for literacy in mathematics. With machines available to carry out routine computations, mathematics learning is no longer confined to the simple mechanics of arithmetic. Children can learn more deeply about the meaning and uses of numbers. They can deal with the properties of space and time, and how to measure them. Mathematical creativity will develop along with the skills.

In the first years of life children have a greater capacity for learning than they will ever have later. By the age of five they can speak their native language fluently and grammatically, using a vast vocabulary. All this has been acquired informally by interaction with parents and others.

Five-year-olds also have mathematical ideas. They can count, they make comparisons on the basis of size, weight, or temperature, and they use words to express these ideas.

Parents who are concerned that their children use language well can help them to do so at this stage. They can also provide many opportunities for doing mathematics with their children.

Parents and early grade teachers can lay a good foundation for any child's later success in mathematics. You don't need a mathematical background. You don't need to buy expensive materials and equipment. You don't even need a lot of time, just a few minutes now and then while you and your child are doing daily chores, going for a walk, or playing games. Grandparents, older sisters and brothers, and baby-sitters can participate.

Some people say, "I don't have a mind for math." We know now that every person has a mind for math, provided the math is presented in an understandable manner. Research has shown that children of all ethnic backgrounds, girls as well as boys, are equally capable of learning mathematics. The games in this book will help you clarify many mathematical concepts for your child, and for yourself as well.

With your interest and warmth, your awareness of the opportunities and of the needs of the child under your care, you can help your child to grow up confident in his mathematical competence.

I.

What Parents Can Do

KNOW HOW CHILDREN LEARN

Children go through stages as they become aware of the world around them. During the first year or so, a child's understanding is based upon direct encounters with people and objects. At a later stage a child comes to know symbols such as words and pictures, and can recall previous experiences. Dealing with abstractions on an intellectual level is a still higher stage of learning. This developmental process takes several years. No stage can be skipped.

The acquisition of concepts requires both maturity and an adequate background of experience for the task at hand. Parents and teachers can present the opportunities for learning, but the actual learning takes place only when the child is ready.

Some children go through these stages more rapidly than others. What makes the difference? Two factors are extremely important, and both are supplied by parents and other caregivers. These factors are the right kinds of experiences at the right time, and the language that accompanies these experiences.

PROVIDE EXPERIENCES

In every culture children observe and imitate the world around them. As a preschooler I watched my father keep

1

records for our small stationery store, and demanded my own notebook in which I, too, wrote rows and columns of figures.

You can provide the kinds of activities that are meaningful at a child's stage of development and appropriate to her current stock of knowledge. Develop an eye and an ear for doing math in a casual way as the need and the opportunities arise.

The process of solving a problem is even more important than getting the right answer. Help your child to see the main aspects of each task. Break down a difficult problem into simpler parts. Question your child, and encourage her to ask questions.

The following experiences with five-year-old Sara illustrate some of these points.

The first time we played More or the Same? (Game 15, page 69), she insisted that an empty glass standing on a thick block could hold more milk than an identical glass set on a thin block. When she placed both glasses directly on the table, as I suggested, she said that they could both hold the same amount. But as soon as she replaced them on the blocks, she reverted to her first answer—the higher glass could hold more. Her contradictory responses seemed not to trouble her, and I did not try to correct her.

Later she watched as I poured milk into both glasses and placed one higher than the other. After several such experiences, Sara concluded that both glasses held the same amount no matter where they were placed.

A few weeks later we played Which Holds More? (Game 16, page 70). I had prepared a pitcher of juice, two identical wide, squat tumblers, and one tall, narrow tumbler. I poured juice into the two short glasses until she agreed they both held the same amount.

Then I poured the juice from one squat tumbler into the tall, thin glass. "Which glass would you take if you wanted a lot of juice?" I asked. She pointed to the tall one.

She poured the juice back and forth several times, changing her answer each time. Finally she thought it through. "That glass is higher...but it's the same juice!"

That was as far as she could go with her explanation. I tried to point out the difference in the width of the two glasses, but Sara did not understand. She was not yet ready to consider that aspect of the problem.

The learning process is a spiral that leads ever upward. Perception of the environment through the tactile, visual, and other senses leads to certain generalizations. These in turn are tested by further explorations in the real world. The new experiences enable a child, in time, to correct the original conclusions and thereby to attain higher levels of understanding.

PROVIDE THE LANGUAGE

Children must eventually acquire the appropriate language to describe their experiences, to organize their thoughts. Here the parent or teacher plays a crucial role. Your conversation with your child directs her attention to the task and helps her to plan her strategy.

Language should be part of the activity—*talk* while you and your child are playing games. Ask questions that encourage your child to describe her actions and explain her conclusions. Your language should be appropriate to your child's level of development, but don't be afraid of an occasional big word—children enjoy them! Use new words casually when you are talking to your child. Over a period of time she will learn what they mean.

Children use words before they understand their exact meanings and the concepts behind them. The mastery of the concept of counting comes long after a child has learned to rattle off "one, two, three, four, five." We must distinguish between rote memorization and true understanding.

Many words and expressions are confusing. The gray cat is bigger than the black cat, but smaller than the dog—in other words, both big and small at the same time. An object can be in front of a child at one moment and in back of her the next moment, depending upon the direction she faces.

Word problems are usually a source of difficulty in school. You can lay a good foundation for your child's future success in this area. In fact, the ability to verbalize when solving math problems generally carries over to other subjects as well.

HOW DO YOU KNOW THAT YOUR CHILD HAS LEARNED?

Repeat the games over and over again, in different contexts and with different materials, until your child has learned the concepts.

How do you know when your child has learned? Observe her actions and listen to her conversation, both while she is playing the games and in her independent activities. Does she understand that concept when it is applied in a different setting? Can she answer appropriate questions about her conclusions, consistent with her language ability? A right answer does not always indicate knowledge. A wrong answer requires further investigation. The following incident and discussion illustrate these points.

I was invited to have dinner at a friend's house while she was enjoying a visit from her grandchildren. My friend set out the seven dinner plates in their proper places on the table. Little Jonny and I offered to help set the table.

"Jonny, how many knives do you need?" I asked. His grandmother had told me that he had trouble with numbers bigger than five.

Slowly Jonny walked around the table, touching each dish in turn as he counted aloud. "Seven knives," he announced.

I observed his activity carefully as he went about the job. If he had been totally unable to count seven objects, I would have given him more practice with smaller sets. On the other hand, he might have made a minor error, like counting the first plate again at the end, or omitting the word "seven," thus getting a total of eight. In that case I would have given him the eight knives he requested, and let him discover that he had one too many. Then Jonny and I could have discussed the reason for the leftover knife. How many knives did he really need? Where had he made a mistake?

BE AWARE OF THE MATH AROUND YOU

Many of the games in this book utilize ordinary household activities. Sorting the laundry, setting the table, preparing food, shopping, fixing things, all afford opportunities for doing math while engaging your child in useful tasks. The job may take a little longer at first, and there will be mishaps. But the outcomes in terms of your child's experience and sense of accomplishment are worth all the effort.

One example is food preparation. This activity develops many mathematical skills, such as counting, measuring liquid and dry substances, weighing, sorting, dividing, estimating, telling time, learning shapes, and recording.

Cooking is a useful skill for boys as well as for girls. How well I remember getting up late now and then on a Sunday morning, to be greeted by a bowl of pancake batter that my son had prepared. (His culinary skills have since served him well.)

Food preparation is the setting for some of the games.

No doubt you will think of many others. In fact, a whole mathematics curriculum can be organized around that one subject!

WHAT ABOUT WRONG ANSWERS?

An incorrect response may mean that your child has solved a different problem from the one you posed, or has not had sufficient experience with simpler activities, or that she has not yet reached the required level of maturity. Or it may just be the wrong time of day, the wrong moment in your child's life.

Ask your child how she arrived at her conclusion. Can you suggest another activity or pose another question that will tell you whether she has really understood?

If one approach doesn't work, guide her to try another. Help her to develop the ability to test her results herself, without having to look to an authority figure for approval. In that way she acquires competence and confidence.

Verbal criticism, far from helping your child to understand, may actually have the opposite effect of making her unsure of herself, afraid to try for fear of being wrong. It is not failure itself but punishment for failure that lowers a child's self-confidence. Be loving and supportive no matter what your child does.

Sometimes you yourself may not know the answers. Then you can say to your child, "I don't know. Let's find out."

BE SENSITIVE

The one word that best describes the desirable attitude to be used in relating to children is *sensitive*. Listen to your child. Be aware of her feelings, frustrations, and difficulties. Then you need not worry about doing the wrong thing.

Children have their own individual styles of learning. Some children respond immediately; others like to work things out in their own minds slowly and quietly. Some are patient, while others are easily frustrated. The attention span may be long or short. Some fear competition or challenge; others love it.

Children respond in a variety of ways to problems that are not yet within their capacity. I asked Marsha, aged two and a half, how many balls I held in my hand, as I showed her first one, then two, and then three balls. She answered correctly for one and two. Three balls presented some difficulty, but Marsha solved it in her own way. She snatched one ball out of my hand and exclaimed, "Two!" She was giving me the message that she was not yet ready for three.

Respect your child's urge toward independence. When she says, "I want to do it myself," you know that she has the self-confidence and motivation to tackle a new learning situation.

Role models are important to a child. You are the one who can help her to develop a positive attitude toward mathematics. If math was your poorest subject in school, don't let it show. This is your chance to start all over again with your child. You can both have a wonderful time playing the games.

Sometimes your child will want to play when you are too busy or too tired. Tell her you will spend time with her later. Be specific—say "after dinner"—so that she doesn't become impatient.

Children don't require material rewards. Learning is its own reward!

Please don't push—that is the cardinal rule. Always be sensitive to your child's attention span, feeling, abilities, and interests. Learning is a creative, happy experience. You don't want to turn your child away from it!

II.

How to Play the Games

The games are arranged in three strands: Shape and Space; Sorting, Comparing, and Measuring; and Number. Each strand is graded according to difficulty. The first Early Games are suitable for children of age two, while the games at the end of each sequence should challenge seven-year-olds.

Chapters 1 and 2 tell you how to play the games and what you can expect of your child. The introduction to each section or chapter in chapters 3 through 6 gives specific information about the concepts in those games.

After you have read the introductory material, read through the games in that section or chapter. Begin by playing those games that you consider most appropriate to your child's present ability. It is best to start with activities in which your child is sure to succeed.

Glance through all the games, including those you think are too elementary for your child. They may contain ideas that you will want to adapt to his present level.

Alternate the games in the three strands. Play one or two Shape and Space games. Then play a game or two in the next strand. At the same time continue to work with the concepts and vocabulary in the games that you have already tried, using different materials and different situations.

Later try a Number game or two. Also continue to play variations of the previous games as long as your child shows interest. Perhaps your child will invent his own versions of the games.

FORMAT OF THE GAMES

What You Need
Have all the materials ready before you start. Feel free to substitute other materials that will lead to the same learning outcomes.

How to Make
Some games include directions for making your own materials. Let your child participate; the workmanship need not be perfect. Involvement motivates a child to use the materials because they are "my own."

Save your grocery cartons and file folders for the games that call for sheets of cardboard. The styrofoam trays in which some stores package fresh fruit and vegetables provide a sturdy and attractive alternative.

Have on hand either a centimeter ruler or a combination centimeter–inch ruler.

How to Play
Some games include suggestions for conversations with your child as you are playing. They guide you in engaging your child's interest, in pointing out what he is to look for, and in knowing what you can expect of him. Of course, you will adapt your language to the needs of your individual child.

What Else Can You Do?
These suggestions for further activities on the same theme will give you ideas for making up still others. Teach your child games from your own childhood, or how to count

in a foreign language. Your input is particularly valuable just because it is yours.

TIME AND SEQUENCE

Devote just a few minutes at a time to each game, but do play them often.

Be patient with your child. Let him stay with a game for as long a period as he is interested. You might suggest a variation after a while, or else come back to it after doing some other activities. Remember that learning is a slow process.

The sequence of the games is not to be followed strictly. For example, your child may not be ready to write numerals at the time suggested. Make a note to come back to that topic later. Children need a tremendous amount of experience with concrete materials before they are ready for abstractions.

MATERIALS

See the Appendices for lists of "beautiful junk," commercial materials and suppliers, commercial games, books, songs, and records.

Several of the suggested homemade games have commercial counterparts. It is a good idea to start with your own, then buy the commercial version later, if you need to.

Keep the "beautiful junk" in appropriate containers, with a place designated for each type of material.

Give your child lots of time for free play with any new toys or materials. He must have a chance to learn about them in his own way, to feel them, sort them, pile them up and knock them down, to learn their shape, color, texture, and weight. Introduce just a few new items at a time. When your child becomes bored with them, store them away for another occasion.

CREATIVITY, IMAGINATION, FUN

Whenever possible, make the game an occasion for imaginative play. Although the directions may call for three bowls, it might be more fun to play with three dolls or three spaceships, depending upon your child's interests. Make up a story or a song to accompany a game, and encourage your child to invent his own. Act out a situation. Let a hand puppet give directions and interact with your child. Riddles are fun, and it doesn't matter if he doesn't guess correctly. You yourself can make an error on purpose, as long as you both know it is just for fun.

Your child may want to change some of the games, or even invent better ones. Give him credit for his invention, and refer to the game afterwards as "Jimmy's garage game." He should be free to explore many situations. He need not be restricted to activities that are supposed to be appropriate for his age, or those that are based on previous learning.

Doing math can be a sociable experience. Share the responsibilities with other parents or caregivers. Involve your child's playmates. Older siblings enjoy taking over, too, and can do a beautiful job.

Your child will be off to a good start in mathematics. More than that, the games will provide many enjoyable experiences for both you and your child, helping to bring you closer together.

III.

Early Games

SHAPE AND SPACE

Introduction

Children's first mathematical experiences involve shape and space. Activities such as going *outside* and falling *down* orient them in space.

Children are aware of the roundness of a three-dimensional ball before they can understand the more abstract notion of the two-dimensional circle that outlines the top of a can. Give them many opportunities to feel, see, and otherwise experience through the senses all kinds of shapes and surfaces.

Vocabulary: up, down, outside, inside, top, bottom, above, below, to the side, open, closed, round, straight, sharp, point, corner, flat, smooth, bumpy, etc.

Games

1. *Up and Down*

How to Play:

Hold the child's hands and walk around in a circle as you sing or chant:

Ring around a rosie,
A pocket full of posies,
Ashes, ashes,
All fall *down*.

Fall down on the last line. Next time change the words of the last line to:

Put your hands *up,*

as you and your child raise your arms.
What Else Can You Do?
* Make up other words for the last line, like "Put your foot up," or "All sit down."
* Talk about "up" and "down" when you walk up and down the stairs.
* Let your child look at herself in a full-length mirror as she puts her hands up, or falls down.

2. *Follow the Leader*
What You Need:
A piece of rope at least four meters (about thirteen feet) long

How to Play:
Lay the rope on the floor to make a closed shape.
"We are going to play Follow the Leader. You must walk in back of me and do whatever I do. This rope is a fence around our yard (or park, or room). Now I am walking inside. Are you walking inside?...Yes, you are walking inside.

"Now let's walk outside. I will cross the fence. Did you cross the fence?...Yes, we both crossed the fence. We are both outside. We are walking outside the yard.

"Now I will walk on the fence. Can you walk on the fence? We must be careful not to fall off the fence.

"Let's go inside again. I will cross the fence. Did you cross the fence? Now we are inside."

Change the shape of the "fence" so that there are two adjoining yards, or there is an opening in the "fence."

Take turns, with your child being the leader.
What Else Can You Do?

• Use a piece of string about one meter (forty inches) long as the fence, place it on the table, and have your child trace it with a finger. Talk about the inside, the outside, crossing from the inside to the outside, walking on the fence.

3. *Mommy (or Name of Caregiver) Says*
How to Play:

This is another game like Follow the Leader. Stand beside your child as you play.

Say "Mommy says put your hand in front of you," as you extend one arm. "That's fine, you put your hand in front of you, just as Mommy said."

Use other directional phrases, like "in back of," "to this side," "up," and "down." Some of these concepts are difficult because the direction depends upon the person's point of view.
What Else Can You Do?

• Face your child as you give the directives.
• Let your child give the directives: "Tommy Says."

4. *Balls and Boxes*
What You Need:
A ball and a box

How to Play:

Pick up the ball.

"This is a ball. Feel how round it is. Now I will roll it to you. Catch the ball....Can you roll it back to me?"

Put down the ball and pick up the box.

"This is a box. It has sharp corners—feel them. It has sharp edges. Feel this sharp edge, and now feel this sharp edge. Here is another sharp corner. Can you find another corner?...Can you find another edge?

"This part of the box is flat. Feel how flat it is. Can you find another flat side?...A sharp corner?...A sharp edge?" (The tactile experience is more important than the words.)

"Can we roll the box?...No, the box doesn't roll. I can push it to you if I push hard....Can you push it back to me?"

Put down the box and pick up the ball again.

"Is this a box? Does it have sharp corners?...No, it is round all over. This is a ball. The ball can roll."

Help your child to find other boxes of various shapes and sizes. Ask her about the sides, edges, and corners.

Help your child to find other round objects—apples, beads, etc.

5. *Cans*

What You Need:

Two grocery cans

How to Play:

Pick up the can.

"This is a can. It has beans (or whatever) inside. Feel this flat side. Here is another flat side. This part is round—feel how round it is.

"Can you make the can roll?...Yes, you made the can roll. Now I will stand it up this way. Can you make it roll now?... No, it won't roll when it stands on the flat side."

Pick up the other can. "Here is another can. Can you show me where it is flat?...Where is it round?...Can it roll?"

Help your child to find other objects that are like cans, such as wheels, checkers, cylindrical blocks, spools. Help her to test each one, as you did in this game.

6. *Matching Balls, Boxes, and Cans*
What You Need:

A ball, an orange, two types of boxes, one can, one spool (or objects similar to these)

How to Play:

Pick up the ball, and give it to your child.

"Can you find something else here that is round like this ball?...Yes, the orange is round. It has the same shape as the ball. Can you roll the orange?...It rolls like a ball."

Repeat this procedure with the boxes and can-shaped objects.

What Else Can You Do?

• Find other objects that have round sides or sharp corners. Look at furniture and toys from this point of view.

• Find objects that are combinations of several simple shapes.

• Examine objects that have irregular shapes. Ask your child to feel them, and discuss flat and round surfaces, sharp pointy corners, sharp edges, and other features that your child can feel.

7. *Find the Shape*

What You Need:

A small ball, a small box, a small can, a large bag

How to Play:

Place all the objects in the bag, after your child has seen them.

Ask her to take out a ball, without looking. How does she know it is a ball? Ask her appropriate questions, as in the previous games.

Then replace the ball, and ask her to take out a box. Repeat the procedure with the can.

Then it is your turn to take out what your child suggests. You might make a mistake in fun. "Oh, isn't this a ball? (as you take out a box)...Let me try again."

What Else Can You Do?

• Use the same materials—a small box, a small ball, a small can. Ask your child to place her hands behind her back, and turn her back to the objects. Place one of them in her hands. Ask her to describe the shape in her own words: "like a can" or "like a ball." Then let her look at the object to confirm her answer.

8. *Will It Fit?*
What You Need:
    Several containers of varied shape and size; several objects of varied shape and size

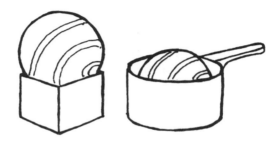

How to Play:
    "Here is a box and here is a pot. You can put things into them. Do you think that ball will fit into this box?...It will fit? Try to put the ball into the box...No, it doesn't fit. Why not?...That's right, the ball is too big. Do you think it will fit into this pot? You think it will fit? Try it. You were right, it does fit into the pot."
    Continue with the other objects and containers.
What Else Can You Do?
    • Use containers with lids, or boxes that close. Ask your child whether the object will fit into the container so that the container can be closed after the object has been placed in it.

    When your child has successfully completed this section, go on to chapter 4, "Shape and Space Games."

SORTING AND COMPARING

Introduction

Learning mathematics requires the ability to recognize likenesses and differences, and to sort objects accordingly. Young children generally sort on the basis of function (things to eat or to wear), categories such as children or dishes, color, form or shape, and personal likes and dislikes.

Later, children learn to compare objects on the basis of such properties as size, capacity, and weight. They need a great deal of experience with the vocabulary that describes these relationships. For example, we use the word "more" in many different contexts in ordinary conversation, and a child may be confused about its exact meaning in a game.

These early experiences lay the basis for the measurement games in chapter 5.

In this book we shall use the familiar word "weight" even when the term "mass" would be scientifically correct.

Vocabulary: big and little, long and short, tall and short, high and low, wide and narrow, heavy and light, dark and light, hot and cold, loud and soft, hard and soft, etc. Bigger than, smaller than, more than, less than, the same as, etc. Biggest, smallest, etc.

Games

1. *Matching*

What You Need:

A pair of socks, a pair of shoes

How to Play:

Place all the objects on the table. As you hold up one sock, say "Can you give me another sock like this sock?... Yes, these socks are the same."

Pick up a shoe, and repeat the procedure.

Then, holding a shoe in one hand and a sock in the other, say "A sock and a shoe are two different things."

Hold up a shoe and say "Can you give me something that is different from this shoe?" Help your child until he understands the concept and the vocabulary.
What Else Can You Do?

• Repeat the activity with other pairs of objects.

• Repeat the activity with one pair of child's socks and one pair of adult socks. Your child can help to sort the laundry.

• Repeat the game using three pairs of children's socks, having different patterns or colors. Refer to the "red sock."

2. *Kitchen Cleanup*
   What You Need:
   Several identical spoons, several identical forks

How to Play:
Place the unsorted flatware on the table. Ask your child to match those that are the same, and to put them away in their proper places. Discuss how spoons and forks are alike—their function, their shape—and how they are different.

For fun, you might ask "Does the spoon belong here?" as you place it in the fork compartment.
What Else Can You Do?

• Play the game with several teaspoons, several tablespoons, and a large ladle.

3. *Toy Cleanup*
   How to Play:
   When it is time to put away the toys, say "Let's pick up all the blocks and put them away." Discuss how to put them away in an orderly fashion. It is a good idea to have a specific place for each type of plaything.

4. *Sorting the Laundry*
   What You Need:
   Many items of clothing, some belonging to your child, and some belonging to another member of the family. Include several pairs of socks.
   How to Play:
   "Some of these clothes are yours, and some are Daddy's. Let's put your clothes here, and Daddy's there.... Whose shirt is that?... Where does it belong?... What are you holding now?... Where does it go?...."
   Help the child to sort each pile according to the type of clothing, and to pair the socks.
   Increase the number of items as your child becomes more skilled in sorting.

5. *Which is Bigger?*
   What You Need:
   One large and one small potato (or apple, etc.)

   How to Play:
   "Tammy wants a big potato, and I want a little potato. Tell me which potato to give to Tammy.... Yes, that's the big potato.... That potato is bigger than this potato."

Repeat with many other objects. Then talk about the "smaller" object.
What Else Can You Do?

• Give your child several identical large envelopes, several identical small envelopes, and two boxes. Ask him to place the large envelopes in one box and the small envelopes in the other box.

6. *Who Is Taller?*
How to Play:

"Let's see who is taller, you or Alan. Stand back to back so that we can measure.... Alan is taller than you.

"Now let's see who is taller, you or your teddy. Hold the teddy so he stands on the floor.... You are taller!"

Later use "short," "shorter than," "as tall as."
What Else Can You Do?

• Build a tower of blocks. Ask your child to build a taller tower, or a shorter tower, or a tower that is just as tall as yours. Discuss how he can judge.

7. *See How I Grow!*
What You Need:

Strip of masking tape about 5 cm (2 in) wide and 1.5 m (5 ft) long
How to Play:

Keep a permanent record of your child's height. Attach the tape to the wall, and mark his height at regular intervals, about every three months.

8. *Which Is Longer?*
What You Need:

Two straws, or two strands of uncooked spaghetti, of equal length
How to Play:

"I want to give you the longer straw. Which straw is longer, or are they both the same?... Yes, they are both the same." If your child is confused, show him that they must be lined up at one end before he can judge.

"Now I will break one straw. Can you tell me which is longer, that straw or this piece?... How do you know?" What Else Can You Do?

• Place two pencils or straws of unequal length in a bag. Ask your child to remove the longer (or shorter) pencil, without looking. Then he can check by comparing the two pencils.

9. *Treasure Hunt*

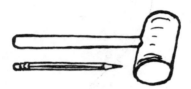

How to Play:

Choose an object such as a pencil or a milk carton. Ask your child to find an object that is longer (or taller) than the chosen object. How does he know that it is longer (or taller)?

Can he find an object that is shorter than the chosen object? How does he know it is shorter?

Can he find an object that is as long (or tall) as the chosen object? How does he know?

If your child cannot tell you or demonstrate how he judged, ask him questions to which he can answer "yes" or "no" or demonstrate his procedure. Give as much help as he needs.

Repeat these activities with many different objects.

10. *Which Is Higher?*
How to Play:

Choose two large pieces of furniture that stand on the

floor, some distance apart, like the kitchen table and a cabinet. Ask your child which is higher. How can he tell? What Else Can You Do?

• Ask your child "What is higher than the kitchen table?" Then it is his turn to ask you to find a higher object than one that he names.

• Play the same game using "lower than."

11. *Which Is Wider?*
What You Need:
    A wide bowl and a tall narrow container
How to Play:
    Place both objects on the table. Ask your child which is taller; which is shorter. Then explain the meaning of "wide" and "wider." If your child is not sure about the meaning of the words used in the previous activities, postpone the use of new words until later.

What Else Can You Do?
• Play Treasure Hunt (Game 9, page 24) using the terms "wider than," "as wide as," and "narrower than." Be sure your child understands the meaning of the words and the concepts. Don't push if the child is not ready. Continue to play Treasure Hunt with the concepts "tall and short," "long and short," "big and little," etc.

12. *Who Is Really Taller?*
    How to Play:
    Let your child stand on a table, so that he appears to be taller than you. Who is really taller?

    Suggest that he place his teddy on a table so that the teddy appears to be taller than he. Who is really taller?

    This game brings out the importance of using the same base line when comparing the height or length of two objects.

    Repeat this game in many different contexts.

13. *Name Another*
    How to Play:
    Choose a category, like things to drink, or things that have wheels, or animals, or friends. Take turns with the child naming things that belong to that category.

14. *I See Something Red*
    How to Play:
    Say "I see a red book. Can you find it?"
    Then it is your child's turn to describe an object in terms of its color, so that you can guess.
    This is a good game to play when you are out walking or driving, or waiting your turn at the doctor's office.
    When your child is ready, you can describe objects in terms of characteristics other than color.

15. *Pouring*
    What You Need:
    Containers of various sizes (children enjoy sets of measuring cups and sets of nesting cans that fit one inside the other); pourable material such as water, sand, rice, dry cereal
    How to Play:
    Give the child many opportunities for free play in pouring from one container to another.

16. *Which Holds More?*
    What You Need:
    Two identical tumblers, milk or juice or water

How to Play:

Show the child the two empty glasses. Tell him you will fill both glasses with milk up to the top. Which glass will have more milk? Or will they both have the same amount?

He can check his answer by filling one glass and then pouring from that glass into the other glass. Help him if necessary.

What Else Can You Do?

• Repeat this game using two identical food cartons or cans, and either liquid or dry pourable material. Children need a great deal of experience of this kind. Talk about "less milk."

• Repeat with two containers that have different capacities.

17. *Which is Heavier?*

What You Need:

Small grocery can and larger, heavier can

How to Play:

Ask your child to pick up each can of food and decide which is heavier. How does it feel to lift each one?

Discuss the terms "heavy," "light," "heavier than," etc.

What Else Can You Do?

• Play "Treasure Hunt" (Game 9, page 24) with heavier and lighter objects.

18. *Tricky Weights*

What You Need:

A large book and an empty carton approximately the same size

How to Play:

Place both objects on the table. Ask your child to guess which is heavier, or are they both the same? How

does he know? Then let him check his guess by lifting each object. Children tend to think that large objects must be heavier than small objects. They need many experiences.

What Else Can You Do?

• Show your child a small container filled with nails and a large empty container, both closed so that he cannot see the contents. Ask him to guess which container is heavier. Then let him check by lifting.

19. *Tall, Taller, Tallest*

How to Play:

Arrange three family members, classmates, or friends in order of their heights. "Mommy is taller than Lisa. Lisa is taller than Tommy. Mommy is the tallest."

Later talk about "shorter" and "shortest," using the same three people.

What Else Can You Do?

• Compare Tommy's height with the height of two children who are shorter than Tommy. Dolls or stuffed animals are also good for this purpose.

• Talk about the three bears in "Goldilocks," using terms like "bigger than" and "biggest," "smaller than" and "smallest," "taller than" and "tallest." Ask your child questions like "Which bear was the tallest? Which bear had the smallest chair? Which bear had the longest bed?"

When your child has successfully completed this section, go on to chapter 5, "Measurement Games."

NUMBER

Introduction

Number is an abstract concept. You can see color, shape, and size. You cannot see number.

The ability to count meaningfully involves many skills. Children must memorize the number words in the correct order (rote counting). Each object must be counted exactly once. Each object has exactly one number word associated with it. The last number word tells how many are in the set. The order of counting doesn't matter; the "number one" object can become the "number four" object on a recount.

How complicated it all is! Yet counting is the basic process in learning arithmetic. A good foundation is crucial.

Children can learn the sequence of number words through chanting, songs, finger play, and other games. Much more difficult is the application of number concepts to collections of objects. It takes a long time for a child to learn to count meaningfully. Do not rush this important process.

Vocabulary: How many, more, less, fewer, another, the same number; names of the numbers.

Games

1. *One Hand, Two Hands*

   How to Play:

   "Can you do what I do?" (Put your hands behind your back.) "I put out *one* hand. . . . Yes, you put out one hand." (Put your hands behind your back again.) "Now I put out *two* hands. . . . And you put out two hands. My two hands can shake your two hands."

   What Else Can You Do?

   • Make up variations. Put out feet or fingers. Touch one ear with one hand, and touch two ears with two hands.

   • After the child has learned the game, stop before you say "one" or "two" and wait for her to say the number.

2. *Verses for Rote Counting*
   How to Play:
   "Can you say (or sing) this with me?

   One, two, three,
   Whom do I see?
   Mary Lou! (Your child's name)

"You can count one, two, can't you?...What comes after two?...Three. One, two, three. Let's say it again: one, two," (pause) "three!...Yes, one, two, three, whom do I see?"

Repeat the verse until the child can chant each line with you.

Here you are teaching your child rote counting. She is simply learning to say the number words in the correct order. This is not the same as counting objects, a much more difficult process.

What Else Can You Do?

• Counting in rhythm helps children to remember the words. Clap your hands, beat a pot lid with a large wooden spoon, or walk in time to the rhythm of the chant or song.

Make up other chants and songs to teach the number words. Be sure that your child has mastered the first few words before you go on to additional numbers. Always recite the whole sequence beginning with one.

There are many counting songs and verses (see Chapter 6).

Here are some original chants:

One, two, three, four,
We are walking (stamping, marching) on the floor.
Jason counts up to four.
1, 2, 3, 4.

One, two, three, look at me.
Four, five, six, I do tricks.
I can count: 1, 2, 3; 4, 5, 6.

One, two, three, four, that's so good I want some more.
Five, six, seven, eight, I will tell you what I ate.
1, 2, 3, 4; 5, 6, 7, 8.
(Say this chant at mealtime.)

One, two, three, four, five,
The bees are in their hive.
Six, seven, eight, nine, ten,
They all flew out again.
1, 2, 3, 4, 5; 6, 7, 8, 9, 10.

It's fun when you and your child take turns saying the number words: you say "one," your child says "two," you say "three," etc. Sometimes children like to count in silly ways. Just relax and enjoy it. You might even join in the fun.

3. *One Cookie, Two Cookies*
What You Need:
A plate of cookies (or apples, or raisins)
How to Play:
Ask your child to give *one* cookie to each person. On another occasion, ask her to give *two* cookies to each person. If she is confused, show her that she can hold one in each hand.
What Else Can You Do?
• When you are setting the table or clearing after a meal, ask the child to bring one spoon or two spoons (forks, etc.).
• Look for occasions when you can ask her to choose either one or two objects from a collection of objects. Ask her how many she wants, and see whether her actions suit her words.

4. *Two Alike*
What You Need:
A heap of unsorted pairs of socks

How to Play:

Pick up a sock and ask, "Can you find a sock like this one, a red and white sock?...You found it! Now we have *two* socks. Find a sock like this blue one....You found it! How many blue socks have we?...Yes, two blue socks. Let's find more socks that are the same, and make more twos."

What Else Can You Do?

• Repeat with other pairs, such as mittens, shoes, boots.

5. *One More, and One More*
   What You Need:
   Five identical cookies (or apples), two plates

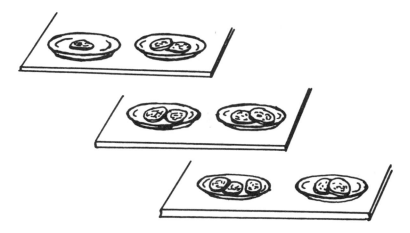

How to Play:

Place two cookies on one plate and one cookie on the other plate. Ask your child, "How many cookies are on this plate?...How many cookies are on that plate?... Which plate has more cookies? Or do they both have the same number of cookies?...Can you fix one plate so they are both the same?"

If your child places an additional cookie on one plate so that there are two on each plate, say "Now I'll put another cookie on this plate. How many cookies are on this plate?...How many cookies are on that plate?... That plate has *three* cookies. Let's count them (as you touch each cookie): one, two, three. Do you know which plate has more cookies?...Can you fix one plate so they are both the same?"

If your child has removed one cookie so that each plate has one cookie, say "I will put one more on each plate," and then continue as above.

What Else Can You Do?

• This game involves real counting of objects. Play it many times with different materials, such as blocks, toys, foods. Make up a story about cars in garages, or any objects that interest your child.

6. *Two Different Things*
   What You Need:
   Three cups, three saucers

How to Play:

Place a cup on a saucer. Ask your child to do the same. Point to a set (cup and saucer) and say "Two things." Ask your child how many things there are, as you point first to the cup and saucer set, and then to the unmatched cup and saucer.

What Else Can You Do?

• Repeat with other groups of two, such as a pajama top and bottom, or slacks and shirt combination, while you are sorting the laundry.

7. *Count Three*

What You Need:

Three spoons, three forks

How to Play:

Place the utensils on the table unsorted. Ask your child to pick up those that are the same. Then ask her how many forks she has. Help her to count, if necessary, pointing to each one as you both say the number words: "One, two, three. Three forks." Then ask her to count the forks by herself.

After she has counted the forks, ask her how many spoons she has. Be sure she understands that the last number word tells her how many spoons she has.

8. *One to One*

What You Need:

Three plates, three spoons (or forks)

How to Play:

This is a good game to play when you are setting the table. Lay out the three plates on the table. Give your child the three spoons, but do not say the number. Say, "Is there a spoon for each plate? How do you know?" Help your child to check by placing a spoon next to (or on) each plate.

Then ask how many plates there are. How many spoons? Is the number the same for both plates and spoons?

What Else Can You Do?

• Give your child more or fewer spoons than the number of plates. Then go through the same procedure as above.

• Ask your child to bring "enough" spoons, forks, and other utensils to match the number of plates.

• Ask your child to set the table for the number of people who will be eating.

9. *Three Every Way*
   What You Need:
   Three small toys (for example, a ball, a car, and a block)

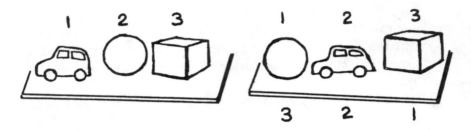

How to Play:
   Ask the child to count the toys. Be sure she can count three objects without difficulty. Suppose she starts with the car.
   Then say, "I will count them a different way. I will say the ball is 'one.' Is that all right?" Count the toys in a different order from the order your child used. Then ask her to count them again in a different order, making the block "one." Be sure to say "three toys" or "three things" after each count.
What Else Can You Do?
   • Ask your child to fetch three spoons from the drawer or any three objects from a larger collection of objects.

10. *Take One Away*
    What You Need:
    6 toy cars (animals, blocks, etc.) Two trays
    How to Play:
    Place three cars on each tray. Ask "How many cars are in this garage?...How many cars are in that garage?...
    "Now watch, this car is driving away. One car drove away. How many cars are still in this garage?... Yes, two cars. And that garage has (pause)...yes, three cars.

"Which garage has more cars?...Which garage has fewer cars?...This garage has fewer cars because two is less than three."

If your child is confused, replace the car and discuss it again, perhaps at another time.

Later continue, "Now another car is driving out of the same garage. How many cars are left in the garage?...Yes, one car. How many cars are in the other garage?...Which garage has more cars?...Which garage has fewer cars?...

What Else Can You Do?

• Terms like "more than," "less than," and "fewer than" are confusing. Your child needs a lot of experience with situations that involve the use of these expressions.

11. *Four, and Later More.*

When your child can play the preceding games without help, repeat Early Number Games 5-10 with four objects. At the same time continue practice with one, two, and three objects.

Please don't rush. By going at a comfortable pace, you are laying a good foundation for your child's mathematical future.

When your child has successfully completed this section, go on to Chapter 6, Number Games.

IV.

Shape and Space Games

Introduction

The games presented here hardly exhaust the great variety of activities that can help children to become familiar with the properties of space. Introduce them to such activities as blowing bubbles, shadow play, making string figures, solving mazes, and peering through a paper-towel tube.

Several games in this chapter use a set of homemade geometric shapes. Besides helping children to learn the properties of the most common shapes, these materials offer good opportunities for all kinds of problem-solving.

The final game in the chapter, the construction of model houses found in various cultures, combines the many skills acquired through the games.

Be sure to alternate the games in chapters 4, 5, and 6.

Games

1. *Repeated Patterns*
   What You Need:
   Collection of two types of small objects, differing in size, color, shape, or some other way, such as macaroni and beans, or two sizes of buttons

How to Play:

Place several objects in a line to make a regular pattern. Ask your child what comes next. And after that one? Then ask her to make a pattern for you to follow.

To draw his attention to the important features, you can sing or chant, as you point to each object, "Big, big, small; big, big, small," or "red, red, blue, blue; red, red, blue, blue." Ask him to chant with you as he points to the objects.

What Else Can You Do?

• Give your child large beads or buttons of several different types and a shoelace, and ask him to make a necklace with a repeated pattern.

• Clap or walk to a rhythmic pattern: "short, short, lo-ong."

• Play Follow the Leader with patterns. One person claps in a rhythmic pattern, and the other person imitates it. Vary the dynamics (loud and soft). Improvise instruments (pots, etc.).

• Make a repeated pattern with two or three types of objects. While your child has her back turned, remove one object. Ask him what is missing.

• Look for repeated patterns in fabrics, wallpaper, table settings.

2. *Copy Mine*
   What You Need:
      Several blocks

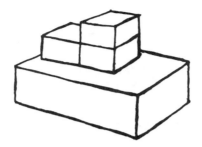

How to Play:

Make a simple block structure. Say to the child, "Guess what I made!...Can you make one just like it?" Suggest that he make a structure for you to guess at and copy.

3. *Mirror, Mirror*
What You Need:
Wall mirror, small hand mirror
How to Play:
Encourage your child to perform movements in front of a mirror, to walk towards and away from the mirror. Ask him what he sees. Suggest that he place the small mirror on or near small objects or pictures, and ask him what he sees.

4. *Balloon Fun*
What You Need:
Balloon, marking pen

How to Play:
Blow up the balloon and paint a face on it. Have your child squeeze the balloon at various places to distort the face.

5. *I Have a Little Shadow*

Ask your child to observe his shadow on a sunny day and note the changes in the direction, shape, and size of the shadow at various times of the day.

Suggest that he hold a book in various positions so that the shape of the shadow varies. Do the same with a frisbee and other objects.

6. *Cans and Boxes*

What You Need:

Several cans, several boxes

How to Play:

Ask your child to trace the top edge of a can with his finger. "That shape is a circle." Ask him to trace the face of a box with his finger. "That shape is a rectangle." Then ask him to find other circles and rectangles.

Later point out the properties of each shape. All circles have the same curved shape, although they may differ in size. All rectangles have four straight edges and four sharp corners. Some rectangles are long and narrow, some are square.

7. *Triangles*

What You Need:

Several cards, scissors

How to Play:

Pick up a rectangular card and ask your child to name the shape. Then cut it along a diagonal. "Are these two pieces rectangles?...Why not?...How many corners does this piece have?...How many edges?...This is a triangle." Cut triangles in other shapes. Ask your child to cut triangles, and to feel the shape with a finger.

8. *"I See a Shape"*
How to Play:
   "I see a circle. It is so big (show with your hands) and it's blue. What is it?" After your child has guessed, it is his turn to pose a question.

Look for examples of various shapes in the environment. Help your child to distinguish between two-dimensional and three-dimensional shapes. An orange is a ball (sphere), but when it is cut you see a circle. What happens to the surface of the milk in a glass when it is tipped? The circle becomes an oval.
What Else Can You Do?
   • Ask your child to sort some of his "beautiful junk" (see Appendix D, page 127) according to shape. He may come up with some surprises!

9. *What's Hidden?*
   Ask your child to hide an object. You will guess what it is by asking questions that he must answer with "yes" or "no." Ask, for example, "Is it longer than my foot?" or "Does it have more than one color?"

10. *Three Stones in a Row*
   In Africa, small children draw this gameboard on the ground.

What You Need:
    Large sheet of paper, pen, three pebbles, three buttons

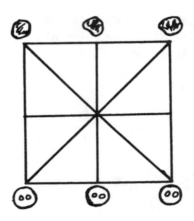

How to Play:
    There are two players, each having three similar counters. Draw the gameboard. The game is played on the nine points at which lines meet.
    The players take turns placing one counter at a time on any point. Each player tries to get three in a row. There are eight ways to do this.
    This game is a good introduction to playing a game by rules.

11. *Three Bugs in a Row*
    This African game is somewhat more difficult than the preceding one. The counters represent waterbugs darting through the water.
What You Need:
    Large sheet of paper, pen, three pebbles, three buttons

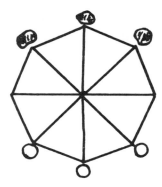

How to Play:

There are two players, each having three similar counters. Draw the gameboard. The game is played on the nine points at which lines meet.

To open, each player places his three bugs on the board as shown. The players take turns moving one bug at a time along a line to the next vacant point. The first player to get three in a row is the winner. There are four winning positions, each going through the center.

What Else Can You Do?

• Play Tic-tac-toe.

12. *Set of Shapes*

Many games in this chapter call for the use of a set of homemade materials called *Shapes.* You and your child can work together to make them. Give him ample opportunity to play with the *Shapes* freely before you introduce the games.

What You Need:

Cardboard or styrofoam sheets (enough for three copies of the pattern shown on page 44)); pencil, ruler, carbon paper, scissors; red, yellow, and blue markers or crayons

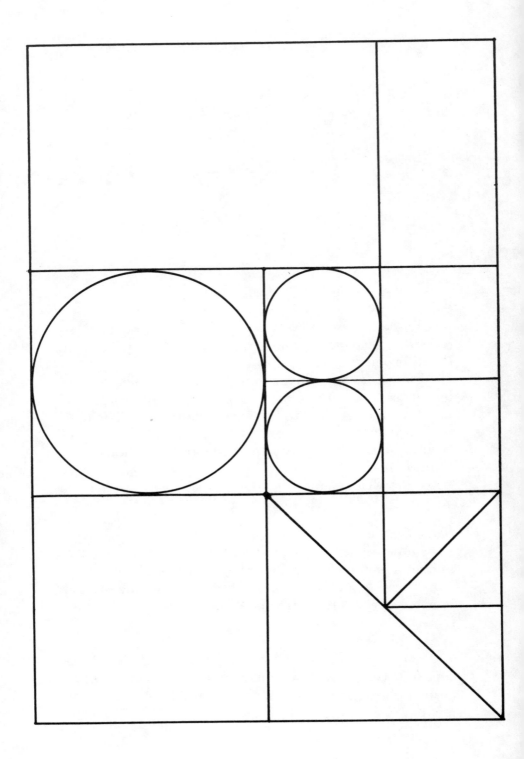

How to Make:

Cut three rectangles to match the one on page 46, or a sufficient number of smaller rectangles. Trace the pattern on each rectangle. Ask the child to color each rectangle on both sides, one red, one blue, one yellow. Cut out the *Shapes*.

An easy way to make a circle is to trace around a jar lid with a sharp knife or pencil.

You will have a set of thirty-nine *Shapes*, thirteen of each color, eight different types, as follows:

1 large circle
2 small circles
1 large square
2 small squares
1 large rectangle
1 small rectangle
1 large triangle
4 small triangles

13. *Copy My Pattern*
What You Need:
    Set of *Shapes*
How to Play:
    Make a simple pattern with red *Shapes*. "Look what I made! Can you guess what it is?... Yes, a snowman. Can you make a blue snowman just like mine?" Then ask the child to make a pattern for you to copy.
What Else Can You Do?
    • Play Repeated Patterns, Game 1, page 39, using the set of *Shapes*. Children enjoy especially discovering which *Shape* is missing when one has been removed from a repeated pattern. You can play similar games with playing cards and *Shape-cards* (see Playing Cards, Game 14, page 89).

14. *Find Another*
What You Need:
　　Eight different *Shapes* of the same color
How to Play:
　　Hold up a *Shape* and say, "I have a circle. Can you find another circle?" After the child has found another, discuss how the two circles are different (size) and how they are the same. Repeat with other *Shapes.*
　　Later start with sixteen *Shapes,* eight red and eight yellow. Now you mention two attributes as you hold up a *Shape:* "I have a small triangle. Can you find another?" or "Can you find another small yellow *Shape?*...Yes, there are three other small yellow *Shapes.*" In this way you draw the child's attention to the attributes of shape, color, and size.
What Else Can You Do?
　　• Play similar games with playing cards or *Shapecards.*
　　• Choose a *Shape* at random, and ask the child to find another that is the same in some way. How are they the same? Are they also different in some way?

15. *Sort the Shapes*
What You Need:
　　Ten or more randomly chosen *Shapes* or playing cards
How to Play:
　　Ask your child to sort the *Shapes* into several piles, using any basis he wants. Then ask him why he sorted them that way. How many are in each pile? Can he sort them a different way and get a different number of piles, or have a different number in each pile?

16. *Hidden Shapes*
What You Need:

Two of each *Shape:* circle, triangle, square, and nonsquare rectangle; large bag or box
How to Play:

The purpose of this game is to help children distinguish different shapes by touch. Start with two shapes that are most dissimilar, as follows:

Place two circles and two rectangles in the bag. Ask your child to reach in, and, without looking, take out a circle. How did he know it was a circle? Replace the circle, and ask him to remove a rectangle.

Repeat with circles and triangles, squares and triangles, and squares and rectangles (a square is a special rectangle).

Later place three different shapes in the bag, and then all four shapes.

17. *The Case of the Missing Shape*
What You Need:

Eight different *Shapes* of the same color

How to Play:

"I will hide one *Shape,* and you tell me which one is missing." Encourage the child to sort the remaining *Shapes* in an orderly fashion.

Later play with a larger collection of *Shapes.*
What Else Can You Do?

• Play What's Hidden, Game 9, page 43, with a *Shape.* Ask questions like "Does it have four corners?"

18. *Shape Trains*
    What You Need:
        Six square *Shapes,* one small and one large of each color
    How to Play:
        Discuss the likenesses and the differences among the squares. Then say "Let's make a *Shape* train. I will start with a big blue square. The next car must be different from this car in just one way. Which square will you choose? You may place it on either side of this one."

    Later, play the game with a larger set of *Shapes*— for example, circles and squares in two sizes and two or three colors. Before you start to play, discuss the features to look for.

19. *Missing Link Shape*
    What You Need:
        See Game 18

How to Play:

Select two *Shapes* that differ in two features and place them on the table, leaving a space between them. Ask the child to find a *Shape* that belongs between them to make a train, as in Game 18. Is there more than one choice?

20. *Shape Combo*
    What You Need:
        Shapes, writing paper, pencil

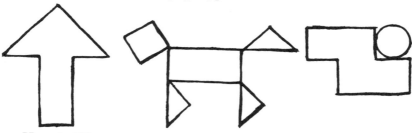

How to Play:

Trace on paper the outline of a pattern you have made with a combination of *Shapes*. Ask the child to fill in with *Shapes*. Can it be done in more than one way?

21. *Shape Cover-up*
    What You Need:
        Complete set of *Shapes*, writing paper; red, blue, and yellow crayons

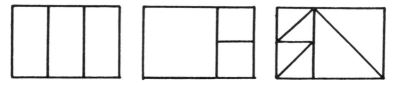

How to Play:

Give your child a large rectangle. Can he cover it completely with one type of smaller *Shape*? How many does he need? Place another large rectangle on the table.

Can he cover this rectangle in a different way, with one type or a combination of types? In how many different ways can a large rectangle be covered?

Repeat with other *Shapes*. Help your child to record the activity on paper by tracing or copying the *Shapes* and coloring them. This game is an introduction to the concept of area.

22. *Tiling with Shapes*
    What You Need:
    Set of *Shapes*, lid of a shoe box

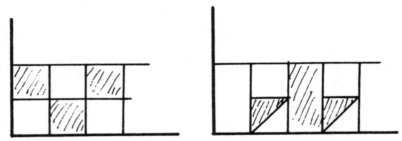

How to Play:
    Ask your child to make a repeated pattern inside the box lid. You may want to start with just the small squares. Then ask him to make patterns with any *Shapes*. Look for repeated patterns in the environment.

23. *Make It Bigger, Make It Smaller*
    What You Need:
    Set of *Shapes* (omit the rectangles)
    How to Play:
    Make a pattern with large *Shapes*, and ask the child to make a copy with small *Shapes*. Then reverse the procedure. An alternative is to draw and color a *Shape* pattern, and ask your child to copy it with small *Shapes* and with large *Shapes*.

24. *Shape Arrays*
What You Need:
At least twelve small square *Shapes,* paper, pencil

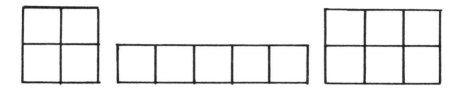

How to Play:
Can your child form a rectangle having two or more rows, using four squares? Five squares? Six squares? Which of these rectangles are square? Help him to keep a record of his discoveries, perhaps by drawing them on grid paper.

25. *Tangrams*
This ancient Chinese puzzle has become popular in the United States.
What You Need:
The following *Shapes:* two large triangles, two small triangles, one small square; material to make two additional *Shapes*

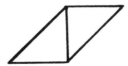 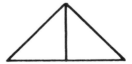

How to Make:
Place two small triangle *Shapes* together in two different ways to make patterns for a parallelogram and a medium triangle.

How to Play:

The child uses all the tangram pieces to form a square, a rectangle, a right-angled triangle, and designs of people, animals, and various objects.

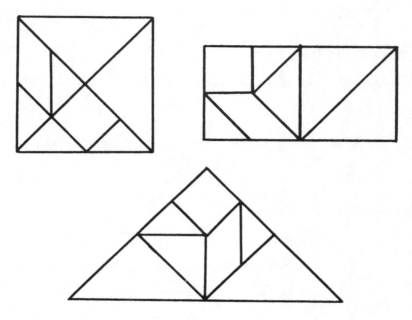

26. *Paper Strip Magic*
    What You Need:

Several strips of paper 5 cm x 1 m (2 in x 1 yd), pencil, adhesive tape, scissors

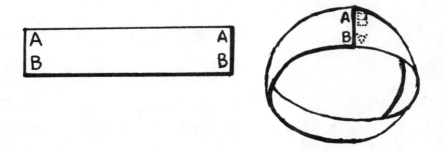

How to Play:

Before taping the two ends of the strip to make a closed band, give one end a half twist. Ask the child to draw a line down the center of the band without picking up the pencil, until he reaches the starting point of the pencil line. There is no need to turn the paper to the other side. Ask him to guess what will happen to the band when he cuts on this penciled line. He will be surprised to see the results! This magic band is called a Moebius strip.

Next time give the end of the strip a full twist before taping the ends together to form a closed band.

Another time draw the pencil line one-third of the way from one edge, and then cut. Try other ways.

27. *Milk Cartons*

What You Need:

Several identical milk cartons, cut down so that all five faces are matching squares; grid paper ruled in 2-cm (or 1-in) squares

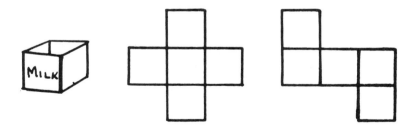

How to Play:

Ask your child to cut the seams of the cartons in as many different ways as possible, to make a flat pattern.

Later, ask your child to draw patterns consisting of five connected squares, in as many ways as possible. How many of these patterns can be folded to make an open box? He can check by cutting and folding.

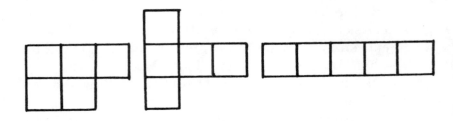

28. *Mirror Magic*
    What You Need:
        Index cards, marking pen, small and large mirrors

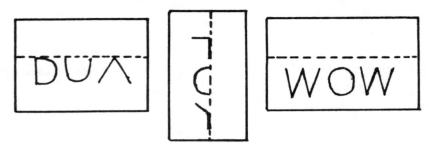

How to Play:
    Copy each of these on a card. Ask your child to hold the mirror upright on the dotted line. What does he see?
    Copy the following on cards, and ask him to hold each card up to a wall mirror. What does he see?
    Can he invent similar puzzles?

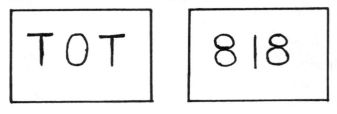

29. *Paper Folding*

The following games illustrate the concept of symmetry.

What You Need:

Paper, scissors, ink, mirror

How to Play:

Fold a sheet of paper in half. Paint a pattern on one side of the fold. Before the ink dries, press the two halves together, then open the paper.

Fold a sheet of paper in half. Cut a pattern along the fold. Open the paper, and place a mirror along the fold line.

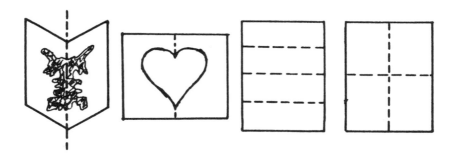

Fold the paper twice and cut a pattern. Here are two different methods of folding into quarters. Can your child predict the pattern before he unfolds the paper?

What Else Can You Do?

• Suggest to the child that he make a mask for Halloween or for a Purim play.

• Make decorations for a Christmas tree or other special event.

• Make symmetrical cutouts to paste on homemade greeting cards.

• Look up directions for origami, the Japanese art of paper folding.

30. *Printed Decorations*
    What You Need:
       One of the following: half potato, styrofoam, spool, or
    sponge; cloth or paper; water-based ink or paint, or a
    stamp pad

    How to Play:
       Your child can use the end of the spool as a pattern, or
    cut a pattern in one of the other materials. Glue styrofoam
    to the end of the spool for convenience in handling. He can
    make repeated designs on cloth or paper and produce
    decorated table mats, kerchiefs, and other objects.

31. *Mapping*
       Make a street map of your neighborhood, and ask
    your child to make models of your house and other
    landmarks to place on the map. Help him trace the path to
    school, etc.

32. *Other Times, Other Places*

Encourage your child to make models of homes in other cultures and other eras—African compound, Eskimo village, medieval castle, Native American pueblo. Look for pictures in books and magazines.

Here are suggestions for an African compound. Some Africans live in round houses with cone-shaped thatched roofs. Several related families live in a compound of many houses, surrounded by a wall.

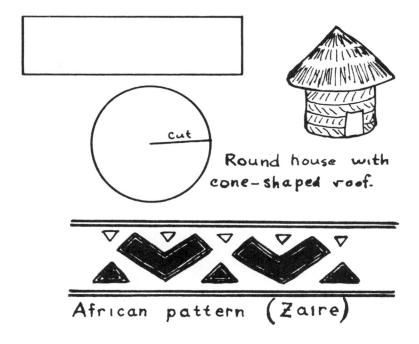

Round house with cone-shaped roof.

African pattern (Zaire)

To make the walls of a round house, glue the two opposite edges of a paper rectangle. To make the cone for the roof, cut along the radius of a circle to the center, and let the edges overlap before gluing. Cover the roof with grass or fringed paper. Decorate the walls of the houses and the compound wall with symmetrical patterns.

Children do imaginative constructions with blocks, paper, and other materials. They can decorate their creations and make floor plans of the layout. This game combines many of the skills that your child has acquired.

V.

Measurement Games

Introduction

The games in this chapter deal with the measurement of length, capacity, weight (mass), and time. The concept of length is considered the most simple, and time is the most difficult because it is most abstract.

Measurement involves the use of number in a continuous sense. Therefore it is more difficult than counting. For example, "there are four dishes on the table" is a simpler idea than "the table is four feet long." (Actually, the length of the table is only approximately four feet, because no measurement is exact, no matter how carefully it is carried out.)

Children are encouraged to carry out measurement activities with informal units, such as their hands and feet, before standard units are introduced. Ask them to "guesstimate" the answer before actually measuring. This leads to skill in estimation.

Standard measurement units are based on the metric system. However, if common units such as the foot and the pound are still in use, by all means introduce them. Look at the school curriculum for guidance. However, once children understand the basic concepts of measurement and have had experience with many kinds of units, the specific units should offer no difficulties.

61

Games

1. *Make Steps*
   What You Need:
   Two identical small spoons, two identical medium spoons, two identical large spoons

   How to Play:
   Give your child one of each type of spoon, and keep the others.
   Arrange your three spoons in size places, using the edge of the table as the base line. "I made my spoons like steps. Can you make your spoons like steps?" Be sure she understands the importance of the base line.
   Ask her questions about the shortest spoon, which spoon is longer than a specified spoon, etc.
   What Else Can You Do?
   • Give your child a shoe. Ask her to find a longer shoe and a shorter shoe, and to arrange them "like steps."

2. *Good Fit*
   What You Need:
   Three envelopes of different sizes, three cards to fit the envelopes
   How to Play:
   Ask your child to put each card into an envelope. Play this game when she is helping to send invitations or greeting cards. Repeat with other materials.

3. *Hidden Objects*
   What You Need:
   Three pencils of different lengths, large bag or box
   How to Play:
   Place the pencils in the bag. Ask your child to reach in and remove the shortest pencil. Have her check by comparing.

   Replace that pencil, and ask for the longest pencil.

   Replace that pencil, and ask for the "middle-sized" pencil.
   What Else Can You Do?
   • Repeat the game, using objects of different weight (mass).

4. *Which Holds the Most?*
   What You Need:
   Three empty containers of the same height, but different capacity (cut milk cartons and other cartons down to the height of a can or pot); sand, dry cereal, water, or other pourable material
   How to Play:
   Point to two of the containers, and ask your child which she thinks holds more. She can check by pouring from one to the other.

   Ask the same question about one of these containers and the third container. Again have her check her response.

   Then ask about all three containers: Which holds the most? The least?

   Repeat this game with many types of containers and materials.

5. *What Does "Big" Mean?*
   What You Need:
   A tumbler, a bowl, a dinner plate

How to Play:

Ask the child to arrange the three objects in size places, from smallest to biggest. Can she tell you why she arranged them as she did? She might look at their height, their width, their capacity, or some other criterion. Or did she change her criterion from one to another?

6. *Seesaw*

What You Need:

Wire hanger, string, small objects

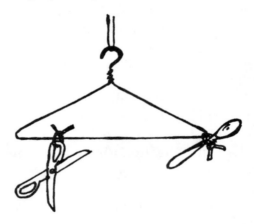

How to Play:

Suspend the hanger so that it can move freely. Attach one object to each end. Ask your child which is heavier. How does she know?

Move the heavier object nearer to the center until the two objects balance each other. Experiment with other positions.

7. *More Steps*
   What You Need:
   Four tumblers of different heights, four cans of different heights

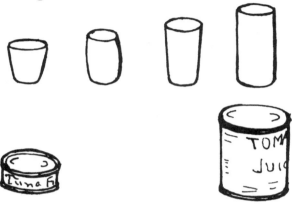

How to Play:
   Arrange the four tumblers from shortest to tallest, "like steps." Ask your child which is the shortest can, which is the tallest can. Place them opposite the tumblers. Then ask your child to fit in the two remaining cans to make steps, like the tumblers. How did she decide?
   Later, use more objects, and give your child less help.

8. *Matching Towers*
   What You Need:
   Eight identical blocks; several objects as tall as a tower of three to six blocks

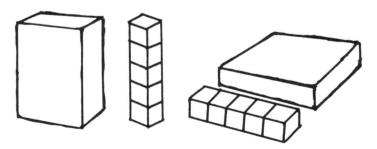

How to Play:

Show your child a box, and say, "If you built a tower as high as this box, how many blocks would you need?" She can check her estimate by building the tower. The box may be "nearly 5 blocks high" or "about 4½ blocks high."

Then lay the box on the table, and ask her to guess how many blocks she would need to build a block train as long as the box. Is her answer the same as for the upright box? If not, let her check with the box in both positions.

9. *Guess the Length*
   What You Need:
      String, scissors
   How to Play:

   Ask your child to guess how long a piece of string would just fit around her waist. Cut the string as she suggests, and let her test her estimate. Then ask her to do the same with your waist. Try it yourself!

   Repeat with many objects—parts of the body, packages, etc.

10. *Telling Time*
    Children become aware of time in relation to the events of the day—time for lunch, time for a favorite TV program. Talk about the hour at which these events

occur, and show your child the position of the hour hand of the clock.

Later explain the position of the hands of the clock at the hour and at half past the hour. The child may say "nearly half past six" or "a little after three o'clock." When you need to know the time, ask *her* to look at the clock and tell you. She will know that you have confidence in her!

Help her to get the "feel" of a five-minute interval, for example, by noting how far you and she can walk in that time. Show her how to time herself on some task or activity by setting a kitchen timer.

When she demands to know, explain "quarter after" and "quarter to" the hour, then five-minute intervals, and finally how the minutes are read.

Show your child various types of clocks and clock faces—pendulum clock, digital clock, faces with Roman numerals. She can make her own pendulum with a weight attached to a string, and discover how the length of the string affects the timing.

The process of learning to tell time takes several years. Be patient!

11. *Get Ready to Measure*
    What You Need:
    Several identical spoons, strands of spaghetti, toothpicks, paper clips, blocks, etc.
    How to Play:
    "How many spoons laid end to end do you think will fit along the edge of this table?" After giving her estimate, the child checks it by laying out the spoons.

    Repeat the procedure with strands of spaghetti. Why is the number different? Try it with paper clips, toothpicks, and other objects. Are they all equally convenient units of measure? What is a good unit for measuring the length of a cracker? The length of the room?

What Else Can You Do?

• Make an outline of your child's body on heavy paper and cut it out. Help her to measure the various parts of her body with the measuring materials used in this game, and to mark the measurements on the cutout. Hang it on the wall.

• Save cardboard tubes from paper towels, and have your child measure large objects by laying the tubes end to end. Compare the length of a bed with the length of the sofa or cabinet.

12. *How Many Cupfuls?*
   What You Need:
      A quart or a liter milk container, five identical cups, dry and wet pourable materials

How to Play:
      Cut off the top of the milk container. Ask the child to guess (estimate) how many cupfuls will fill the container. How can she tell? Let her check by filling that number of cups and pouring into the container.

   Then reverse the procedure. How many cups can be filled from a full quart container? She checks by pouring.

   Repeat the whole procedure with smaller and with larger cups. Why is the number of cupfuls different in each case?

   Repeat with other cups, containers, and materials.
   What Else Can You Do?

• After you and your child have played this game many times, use just one cup and fill it repeatedly.

13. *Will It Fit?*
   What You Need:
   Two containers of different shape, pourable materials
   How to Play:
   Fill one container. The child guesses whether the contents will just fit into the other container, or be too little or too much. She checks her guess by pouring.
   Then fill the second container, and ask the same question. Does her answer conform to her reply to the first question? Again, she checks by pouring.
   Repeat the entire procedure with other pairs of containers, some pairs having the same capacity, others differing in capacity.

14. *Make Them Even*
   What You Need:
   Transparent container, two identical glasses, water or juice
   How to Play:
   Partly fill the container with about one to two glassfuls of liquid while your child is not watching. Then ask her to guess how high to pour the liquid in each glass so that the amounts will be equal. Mark the glass at that level. Then she pours to check her estimate. She may want to change her mind after pouring into the first glass.
   Repeat this game many times with the same container and glasses. Later use more glasses and other containers.
   Try it yourself as your child watches!

15. *More or the Same?*
   What You Need:
   Two identical tumblers, one thin block, one thick block

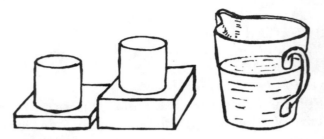

How to Play:

Arrange the tumblers on the blocks, as shown. Ask your child which is the taller tumbler. Which would hold more milk? If your child does not answer correctly, ask her to place both tumblers on the table and observe their heights. Does she say that they are the same height?

Then ask her to replace them in their original positions. Ask again which is the taller; which would hold more milk.

If her answers are inconsistent, have her place both glasses on the table, fill them with liquid, and replace them on the blocks. Do this many times, until she is able to respond correctly.

16. *Which Holds More?*
    What You Need:

    Two identical tumblers; another tumbler that is taller and narrower than the first two; juice or another enjoyable drink

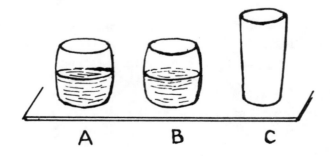

A   B   C

How to Play:

Fill tumblers A and B to the same level. Ask your child whether A or B has more, or are they both the same?

When she agrees they are the same, pour the liquid from B into the tall narrow tumbler C. Say "If you wanted a lot of juice, which would you take, this glass or that glass?" pointing to A and C. Many children say that C has more. Ask her to pour from C into B. Repeat the question.

Repeat the procedure on other occasions, with different tumblers, until she can give the correct response and some justification for that response. Don't expect a scientific explanation!

17. *Whose Foot?*

Units of length were originally based on parts of the body, such as the foot, the hand, and the arm. But with the growth of trade, problems arose. Whose arm should be used to measure cloth, the weaver's or the buyer's? Units of measure had to be standardized. The British yard, for example, was set as the distance from King Edgar's nose to the tip of the middle finger of his outstretched arm.

In the following activities you and your child will begin by measuring in informal units based on the parts of your own bodies. The different outcomes resulting from using an adult foot and a child's foot point up the need for standardization. Then have your child use a standard foot ruler as the unit. Explain that the standard foot was used for many centuries, but now we are changing to other units, part of the metric system (to be discussed in Game 26, page 79). Your child is acquiring the important ability to adapt to any type of measuring unit.

What You Need:

Paper and pencil

Unit		Maria	Daddy
Pace			
Heel-to-Toe			
Handspan			
Palm			

How to Play:

Decide which object will measure—let's say the length of the sofa. Help your child to make a chart in which to record the measurements in both adult and child units based on the pace (normal step), heel-to-toe step, handspan (tip of thumb to tip of little finger), and width of the palm. Add other units, if you like.

What Else Can You Do?

• Make a cutout of your foot and another of your child's foot. Use these units of length to measure various objects. Discuss the need for standard units, then introduce the standard foot ruler (approximately 30 cm).

• Play games like Giant Steps.

18. *String It Along*

What You Need:

String, marking pen, twelve-inch ruler

How to Play:

Have your child measure the length of the table with a piece of string. Then she places the end of the string against her foot, and marks one foot-length on the string.

She folds the string until the remainder is less than a foot-length. The table is about ten feet long, measured in child-feet!

Repeat with other objects and parts of the body. Repeat with a foot (12-inch) ruler.

19. *Two-Pan Balance Scale*
What You Need:

Wire hanger, string, adhesive tape, two identical milk cartons (large)

How to Make:

Bend the hanger evenly at both ends. Use the lower part of each milk container, about eight centimeters (three inches) deep. Cut four lengths of string, each long enough to go around a box twice. Punch a hole in each face of the box, as shown. Thread each piece of string through a hole in the box, the hanger, and the opposite hole in the box, and tie a knot underneath. Pull the box down so that the strings are taut, and wrap tape around the strings above the box.

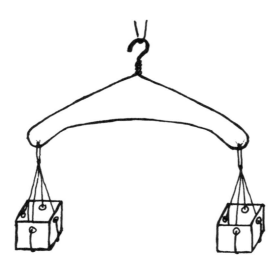

How to Play:

Ask your child to choose two objects and estimate which is heavier. She can check by placing one object in each pan of the balance scale.

Repeat with many objects and combinations of objects.

What Else Can You Do?

• Prepare six identical balls of modeling clay, one of which contains a heavy object hidden within it. Ask your child to find the heavier ball.

20. *How Many Nails?*

What You Need:

Two-pan balance scale, several identical nails, several objects

How to Play:

Ask your child to hold an object in one hand, and enough nails in the other hand to equal the weight of the object. She can check her estimate with the balance scale. She can say "The car weighs five nails." Repeat with the other objects. Ask her to arrange them in the order of their weight. On another occasion she can use heavier or lighter units of weight (mass). Perhaps she can record her results.

21. *Measure in Pucks*

What You Need:

Three plastic containers with different capacities, marking pen or crayon; water or sand

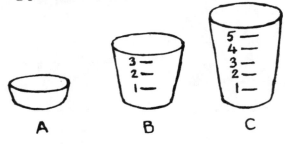

How to Play:

Ask your child to estimate how many times the contents of container A will fill B. She fills A, pours the contents into B, and marks the level on container B. She fills A again and empties into B, marking the second level. She continues until B is full. Then she pours from B into A to check her measurements.

Ask your child to invent a name for the capacity of A—for example, a "puck."

At another time, repeat the procedure with container C, again using A as the unit. She can use these marked containers to play store, restaurant, gas station, and other games.

What Else Can You Do?

• Show your child how to use measuring cups and other calibrated containers for cooking, painting, etc.

22. *Paper Clip Ruler*

What You Need:

A paper clip, pencil, writing paper, a strip of heavy paper about three centimeters (1 in) wide

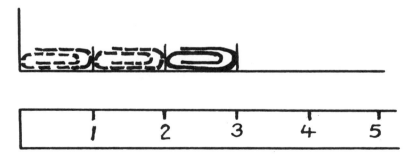

How to Play:

Ask your child to estimate how many paper clips would fit along one edge of the sheet of paper. Can she check her estimate by measuring with just one clip? Help her to place the clip end to end with the paper, marking the end of the clip, and laying it down in the next position, marking it, etc. Can she find an object as long as three clips by measuring it against the marked edge of the paper?

Later suggest that she make her own paper clip ruler on the strip of paper, numbering the units to show the scale. She can measure various objects and make a record of their lengths in paper-clip units.

Is this ruler appropriate to measure the width of a fingernail? The distance to the library?

23. *Making a Graph*
What You Need:

Paper-clip ruler (Game 22, p. 75), several leaves of different lengths, writing paper, pen, string
How to Play:

The child can measure the lengths of a collection of leaves or other objects, and make a graph of the results, as shown here. Check that the length of each bar is accurate by placing the appropriate leaf against it. Is a clip ruler accurate?

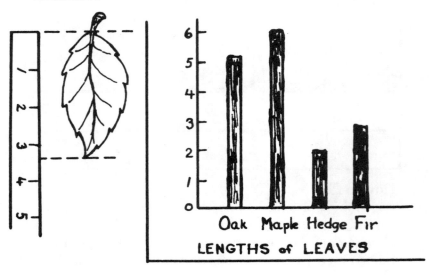

LENGTHS of LEAVES

Your child can compare the perimeters (distance around the leaves) by measuring with string and laying the string along the clip ruler to obtain the length.

24. *Spring Scale*
What You Need:
Length of thin elastic or rubber band (15 cm/6 in), string, paper clip, cardboard rectangle, adhesive tape, spoon or heavy nail
How to Make:
Make a loop at each end of the elastic. Place the opened clip through one loop to use as a hook. Attach the elastic and tape to the cardboard.

How to Play:
Suspend various objects and note how much the elastic stretches.

Help your child to calibrate the spring scale in terms of the weight of a unit like a spoon or a nail. First make a horizontal mark on the tape on a level with the lowest point of the elastic as it hangs slack. Now suspend the spoon from the hook, and mark the lowest point of the elastic. The space between the two marks is one interval. Continue to mark the tape at equal intervals. Label these marks 0, 1, 2, etc.

Your child can use this spring scale and the balance scale (Game 19, page 73) when playing store, house, and other games.

25. *My Own Calendar*
    What You Need:
    Large monthly calendar on which your child may write and draw

How to Play:
Explain the calendar—the sequence of numbers, the days of the week, the months of the year. Talk about birthdays and holidays, and show the dates on the calendar.

When she is ready and interested, suggest that she mark each date with the weather or some event, using words or pictures.

Help her to count the number of days until a future event, using the calendar as a guide. Ask questions like "What will be the date two days from today, when we will visit Grandma? What day of the week will it be?"

Associate years with birthdays. Suggest that the child make a calendar for someone's birthday month.

26. *Standard Units*

Over a period of some time, introduce your child to standard units of length, mass (weight), capacity, and temperature. Give your child a ruler marked in centimeters (with no smaller subdivisions) and a measuring tape, and encourage her to use them in many different ways, keeping records of the measurements. For example, she can make a chart comparing her measurements with those of another family member. Suggest that she "guesstimate"; then measure. (See Appendix A, page 121, for a metric table.)

	Ray	Mom
Height	85 cm	163 cm
Foot length	16 cm	24 cm
Waist	41 cm	75 cm
Small toe	2 cm	3 cm

Show your child various types of scales—in the market, the drug store, the post office, the doctor's office. Help her to keep a record of her weight, perhaps in graph form.

Show her various types of thermometers—oven, body, weather—and explain the scales. How does it feel when the outdoor temperature is 20°C? Or minus 5°C?

27. *Read the Labels*

What You Need:

Packaged and canned groceries

How to Play:

Help your child to read the labels. Understanding the quantities written on the labels often is a challenging task for an adult! Are the measurements in terms of mass (weight) or capacity (volume)? Are the units listed in the metric system or the customary (pound, ounce, pint) system? (See Appendix A, page 121, for information on the metric system.)

28. *Follow the Recipe*

Write recipes that your child can follow:

Breakfast Cereal

1 ounce dry cereal
150 ml milk
1 handful raisins, washed

Put everything in a bowl and eat it.

VI.

Number Games

Counting is the basis for arithmetic. Meaningful counting involves many skills, already described in the introduction to the section on numbers in chapter 3 (see p. 30).

New sources of confusion appear when children begin to use numbers in other ways. There is a great difference between three cups and the third cup on the shelf. The third cup is different from one-third of a cup, and that phrase, in turn, does not mean one-third of a cupful, although they are often used interchangeably.

Written symbols introduce another level of difficulty. Children must learn to associate the written numerals with the appropriate collections of objects. The games also contain suggestions for the use of language for other symbols in arithmetic.

The games encourage the development of the important skills of estimation and mental arithmetic. You can invent many more activities for practicing these skills.

Although the games do not call for a hand-held calculator, its use can lead to valuable mathematical insights. The calculator enables a child to solve problems involving long calculations and to discover interesting number patterns. Besides, it's a wonderful toy.

81

Look for everyday opportunities for your child to practice, but never let math become boring!

Games

1. *"Band of Angels" Counting Song*

You can adapt this simple spiritual to many situations by changing a few words. This version is called "House of Children." See the list of songs in Appendix C (page 125) for further suggestions.

What You Need:

Improvised rhythm instruments: a pot lid and large spoon, sticks, blocks of wood

How to Play:

Chant or sing the verses with a marked rhythm, stressing the underlined words. Meanwhile clap or beat in a steady tempo, as shown by the music notes.

There is <u>one</u>, there are <u>two</u>, there are <u>three</u> little <u>children</u>,
There are <u>four</u>, there are <u>five</u>, there are <u>six</u> little <u>children</u>,
There are <u>seven</u>, there are <u>eight</u>, there are <u>nine</u> little children,
<u>Ten</u> little <u>children</u> in our <u>hou</u>-ou-<u>ouse</u>.

What Else Can You Do? (over a long period.)
- The child marches in time to the beat.
- Vary the tempo for a slow or a fast walk.
- Vary the steps (giant or baby steps).
- Vary the actions. Change the words to suit.
- Use the song for finger play. The last line might be "Ten little fingers on both hands."
- Clap or beat only on the stressed words, while the child walks or claps in time to all the beats (the music notes). Then change places with your child.
- Can you translate the song, or the number words, into a foreign language?

• Count backwards: "There are ten, there are nine, ..." as your child extends or bends his fingers.

2. *Guess How Many*

What You Need:

Several counters (beans, pennies, poker chips)

How to Play:

Hold several counters in your closed fist, and ask your child to guess how many you are holding. Open your hand and ask again how many. He can check his guess by counting.

Take turns with your child.

Use one to four counters until your child becomes adept.

3. *Two-square Trains*

Your child will learn to count pictures of objects, rather than the objects themselves.

What You Need:

Fifteen cards or styrofoam rectangles, each measuring about 6 x 12 cm (2½ x 5 in); red and blue marking pens.

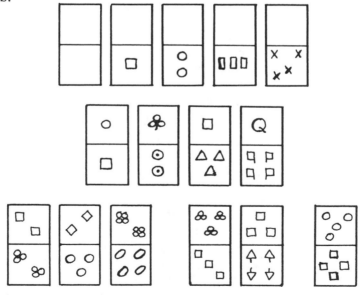

How to Make:

Two-squares are similar to dominoes, but differ in several respects. The shape and the arrangement of the spots are different in each square. Half the *Two-square* has red spots, the other half has blue spots. Your child will learn to recognize a set of three, for example, no matter what objects are represented, or how they are arranged on the card.

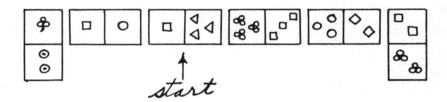

start

How to Play:

Lay out the six *Two-squares* having from one to three spots in each square. Pick up a *Two-square* and say: "Let's make a *Two-square* train. I'll start with this car." Place it on the table. "How many red spots are in this square?... How many blue spots are in that square? ... Yes, this is a One–Three car. The next car on this side must have just one spot in a square. Or you can put a car on that side that has three spots in a square. Which would you like to do?"

Continue to take turns until all the *Two-squares* have been placed on the table.

What Else Can You Do?

• Play with the ten *Two-Squares* having from one to four spots in each square. Say "I am putting down a Two–Four car. I am matching a two to a two."

• After your child has learned the meaning of zero, play with all fifteen *Two-squares*. More than two can play. Instead of arranging the *Two-squares* in a straight line, make a rectangle ("fence") or some other formation.

4. *One Less, Nothing Left*
   What You Need:
   Three folded shirts (or other garment)
   How to Play:
   "How many shirts are in this pile?...If I put one in the drawer, how many will be left in the pile?" Place one shirt in the drawer, and ask your child to count the remaining shirts to check his answer.

   Repeat the question and the activity until no shirt is left. "Yes, none is left. We say the number is zero."

   The concept of zero is a difficult one, even for older children and adults. Give your child a lot of practice.
   What Else Can You Do?
   • Start with a collection of four items. Remove one at a time until zero items remain.
   • Play Guess How Many (Game 2, page 83) with zero counters.
   • Play Two-square Trains (Game 3, page 83) with all fifteen *Two-squares.*

5. *Most and Least*
   What You Need:
   Three dishes or trays, various foods or toys, a hand puppet (you can make one out of a paper bag)
   How to Play:
   Arrange the dishes approximately as follows:

   Dish A has one cookie.
   Dish B has two apples.
   Dish C has three buttons.

   Pretend that you are the puppet. Say in a puppet voice, "I want the dish with the most things. Please give it to me....Thank you.

   "Now you take the dish with one less thing....I have three things. How many have you?...

"Please give Daddy the dish with one thing less than yours. How many things does Daddy have?...You did that very well!"

Ask the child who has the most things? The least? The biggest number of things? The smallest number of things?

What Else Can You Do?

• Play the game with four dishes, having up to four items in each. Have the puppet make an error, so that your child can correct him and explain the right way to do it.

6. *Now Try Five*

Play Four, and Later More (Early Number, Game 11, page 37) and Guess How Many (Game 2, page 83) with five objects, while you continue to practice zero to four.

7. *Nothing Is Least*

What You Need:

Four dishes, various foods

How to Play:

Arrange three dishes as in Most and Least (Game 5, page 85) with this difference: place two *different* items on Dish B, and three *different* items on Dish C. Play as in Most and Least. This time you might role-play "Goldilocks and the Three Bears."

Then introduce an empty dish, saying "This dish is for Goldilocks. How many things does it have? Which is the least?"

8. *The Number Stays the Same*
   What You Need:
       Five or more varied objects
   How to Play:
       Follow the procedure in Three Every Way (Game 9, page 36). Is your child sure that the number remains the same, no matter how the objects are counted?
       Replace one item by something else, and ask him how many things are in the collection. Does the number remain the same?

9. *Number Patterns*
   What You Need:
       Several identical toothpicks

   How to Play:
       Suggest to your child that he make as many different arrangements as possible with two toothpicks. Can he copy them on a sheet of paper?
       Ask him to do the same with three, then four, etc.
   What Else Can You Do?
       • Repeat the procedure with buttons or other objects.

10. *Some Here, Some There*
    What You Need:
        Five spoons
    How to Play:
        Place two spoons on the table and three spoons on the kitchen counter. Ask your child to count the spoons without moving them.

Play this game when he is helping to unpack the groceries. How many cans are on the table? How many in the bag? How many altogether?

What Else Can You Do?

• Play Guess How Many (Game 2, page 83) with two hands. After your child has checked the number of counters in your left hand and the number in your right hand, ask him how many you are holding altogether. You might close your hands again and ask him to "guess" how many are in the two hands together. He can check by counting all the counters. Eventually he will learn the number combinations.

11. *Dominoes*

What You Need:

Standard set of twenty-eight dominoes, or use the *Two-squares* in Game 3 (page 83), and make thirteen additional pieces.

How to Play:

Your child will learn to play a game with rules. Two or more can play. You may want to start with just part of the set, until your child learns to count up to six spots.

Lay the dominoes on the table face down. Each player takes a domino in turn, until none is left. He then sets up his dominoes in front of him so that the faces are not visible to the other players.

The person holding Six-Six starts. Play continues as in Two-Square Trains (Game 3, page 83). If a player cannot match either end of the line on the table, he says "pass," and the next player takes his turn.

12. *Feel How Many*

What You Need:

Shoe box, four small objects

How to Play:

Place the objects in the box. Ask your child to reach in, and, without looking, tell how many objects are in the box. Repeat the game with five or more objects.

13. *Hear How Many*

How to Play:

The child leaves the room and closes the door. He knocks four times, for example.

You ask: "Is that Mr. Three?"

Child: "No."

Adult: "Is that Mr. Four?"

Child: "Yes."

Adult: "Come in, Mr. Four. How are you today?"

Take turns going out and knocking. Vary the number and the rhythm.

14. *Playing Cards*

The card games can be played with a deck, or part of a deck, of ordinary playing cards, or you and the child can make a set of *Shape-cards*. The shapes—circle, square, rectangle, and triangle—match the *Shapes* in Chapter 4. Making the cards is a good joint activity that may stretch over several days.

What You Need:

Twenty-four blank index cards (3 x 5 inches); four marking pens—red, green, blue, black

How to Make:

Make four cards for each number, as shown in the chart. Each of the four cards is marked with a different color and spots of a different shape.

The sample card for each number shows you how to arrange the spots. This arrangement will help the child to recognize the number quickly.

Number	Red	Green	Blue	Black	Sample Card
0					(empty card)
1	○	□	△	▯	card with ○
2	□	△	▯	○	card with □ □
3	△	▯	○	□	card with △ △ △
4	▯	○	□	△	card with ▯ ▯ ▯ ▯
5	△	□	○	▯	card with □ □ ○ □ □

How to Play:

Give your child plenty of time for free play with the cards. Notice what he does with them. Does he build houses, or play football, or sort them?

After a great deal of free play, suggest that he sort the deck, or part of the deck. Then talk to him about his way of sorting. Ask how many cards are in each pile. Can he sort them a different way?

Give him a box in which he can store his deck of cards.

15. *Pairs of Cards*
What You Need:

Shape-Cards (see Playing Cards, Game 14, page 89) or a standard deck of cards

How to Play:

Two or more can play.

At the beginning, play with just a small number of cards, and lay the hands of cards open on the table. Start with two players; more can join when your child knows the game.

Select the ones, twos, and threes. Deal four cards to your child, four to yourself, and lay out four on the table.

The object of the game is to pair a card in the hand with a card on the table that has the same value. If the player cannot make a pair, he must lay one of his cards on the table. It is not necessary to have a winner at this stage. The game ends when each player has played all his cards.

The conversation might go something like this:

Adult: "You have four cards, I have four cards, and there are four cards on the table. Do you have a card that matches a card on the table—has the same number of spots?"

Child: "This card matches that one. They are both black."

Adult: "Yes, both are black. In this game we are looking for cards that have the same number of spots. How many spots are on that card (pointing to a card in your child's hand of cards)?"

Child: "Two spots."

Adult: ""Is there a card here in the middle that has two spots?"

Child: "That red one."

Adult: "Right. Your Two-card and the red Two-card together make a pair. Two cards that have the same number of spots make a pair, just like two socks make a pair. Put the pair in a separate pile next to you. Now it is my turn. I can match this Three-card with that Three-card to make a pair. Now it is your turn again."

What Else Can You Do?

• Use a larger part of the deck. After dealing the first round, place the remainder of the cards face down on the table. Each player picks an additional card from the top of this deck after taking his turn.

• When your child begins to recognize numerals, substitute two numeral cards for two *Shape-cards* of each value. Point out that the double wavy line marks the bottom of the card.

• Each player's final score can be either the number of cards in his pile of pairs, or the total value of those cards.

• Young children can learn simplified versions of Go Fish, Casino, and Old Maid (under a more appropriate name!).

16. *Ten Things*

Give the child many opportunities to count up to ten objects in a collection. You will find many occasions for counting; try, for example, the number of utensils on the table, shirts in the laundry, blocks in a tower, coins in your change purse, or cans (boxes, jars) in the week's shopping.

17. *Finger Counting*

Fingers are the handiest objects—they are always with you! Educators have found that many children resort to finger counting even when it is expressly forbidden, and today the method is being encouraged.

Help your child under your care to learn the most efficient ways of finger counting.
How to Play:

Sing or chant "Band of Angels" (see Game 1, page 82), substituting the word "fingers." The last line might be "Ten little fingers on both hands."

Raise an additional finger for each number as you both sing. Repeat the song many times, sometimes raising the fingers and other times bending them. Say the numbers in reverse order.

Play the game How Many Fingers? Raise several fingers on one hand and say "Can you do this?...How many fingers are up?" Encourage your child to count as he raises them. Remember to include "zero fingers." Take turns with the child.
What Else Can You Do?

• After your child has learned to recognize five fingers without having to count them, play this game. Raise five fingers of one hand and one finger of the other. "How many fingers are up? Can you count the short way? How many on this hand?...Yes, five. What number is after five?...How many fingers altogether?" Continue with the numbers up to ten. Then you call out the numbers, and ask the child to raise the appropriate number of fingers.

18. *What Number Is Missing?*
What You Need:

Six Shape-cards of one color (see Playing Cards, Game 14, page 89), or the cards having values one to five in one suit of ordinary playing cards
How to Play:

Ask your child to lay out the cards in order, according to the number of spots. If you are using ordinary cards, make an additional card for zero. After he has done this correctly, remove one card while he is not looking. Gather the remaining cards into one pile, and ask him to find out which card is missing. Later include higher-valued cards.

19. *Five Questions*
What You Need:
    Several objects in a closed container
How to Play:
    Ask your child to hide several objects in a container; tell him you will guess how many are in the container. He must answer "yes" or "no" to each of your questions. Say "Are there more than three?... Less than eight?" rather than naming specific numbers.

    Take turns guessing. Young children tend to ask "Is it eight?...Is it three?" The concepts of "more than" and "less than" are far more difficult. Don't rush your child.

    After your child has learned the game, limit the number of questions to five, or any other suitable number. Show him how to tick off the five questions on the fingers of one hand. Occasionally ask "How many questions have I asked so far? How many more may I ask?"

20. *Reading Numbers*
    Point out the numerals, the written symbols for numbers, in the child's books and many other places— clocks, food packages, store windows and circulars. Make up games like finding car license plates that start with 3 or end in 7. Write several numerals about 10 cm (4 in) high, and ask the child to trace each one with his finger.

21. *Spot Bingo*
What You Need:
    Five square cards, 15 x 15 cm (6 x 6 in); five

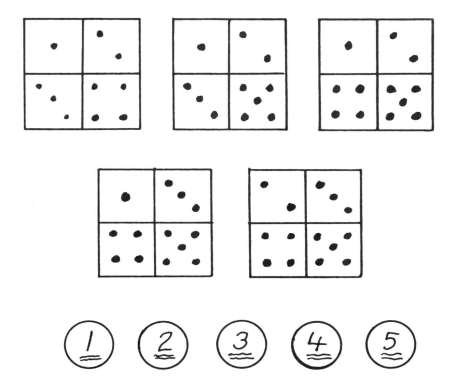

cardboard or plastic discs or squares, 5–7.5 cm (2–3 in) across; marking pen

How to Make:

Subdivide each card into four small squares, and draw from one to five spots in each small square, as shown. Write the numerals from 1 to 5 on the discs. The wavy line under each numeral shows your child how to hold the disc in order to read the number correctly.

How to Play:

Place all the numeral discs into a container. Ask your child to choose a Bingo card. Place it on the table in front of him so that the smallest number is in the upper left corner. Take out a disc, and call the number: "Have you a three?" If he says he has, he covers the Three-square with the disc. Continue until he has covered all four sets of spots on his card. Then change places, and let him call.

He may want to read the numerals and take care of his Bingo card at the same time.

Several children can play, taking turns calling out the numbers. They can place counters (beans, checkers, buttons) on their Bingo cards. The game ends when someone has covered an entire card. Since each of the five cards is different, one child is sure to finish before the others.

What Else Can You Do?

• Make additional Bingo cards, using either sets of spots or numerals from one to nine, as well as discs numbered to nine. Play as before, or make up your own rules. Perhaps your child can invent some new ways of playing.

22. *Five Cents, One Nickel*
What You Need:
   Twenty pennies, two nickels (real money)

How to Play:

Make several unequal stacks of pennies. Ask your child which is the biggest, which the smallest. He can check by counting the pennies in each pile.

Make a stack of five pennies, and ask him to do the same. We call this stack of pennies "five cents." We can exchange the stack for one nickel, which is also called "five cents." Demonstrate as you talk. Relate the group of five pennies to the five fingers on a hand, as shown.

Ask your child to give you change for one nickel or for two nickels.

23. *Making Sums*
What You Need:

Three nickels; twelve pennies

How to Play:

Ask the child to make each of the sums six cents through nine cents in two different ways, and to make ten cents in three different ways.

What Else Can You Do?

• Play the last game in "Finger Counting" (Game 17, page 93). Show the relationship between five fingers on one hand and five cents in one nickel.

24. *How Many More?*
What You Need:

Ten pennies; one nickel

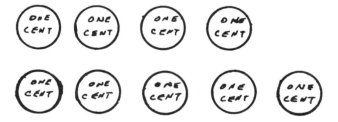

How to Play:

"If you have four pennies, how many more pennies will you need to have a nickel's worth?" Ask your child to place four pennies in a row in front of him. Take a nickel and ask, "How many pennies can I get in exchange for my nickel?" Have him make the exchange, and line up the five pennies in a row opposite his four pennies. Repeat your first question. Your child can count how many pennies he needs to complete his row to match yours.

Ask similar questions about the fingers.

Ask the same questions about zero to five pennies or fingers.

25. *And Even More*
What You Need:

Twenty pennies; two nickels

How to Play:

"If you have _____ pennies, how many more will you need to make two nickels' worth of pennies?" Fill in the blank with various numbers. Follow the procedure in "How Many More?" (Game 24, page 97) to help the child solve these problems. Play similar games with the fingers, and with the other collections of objects.

The ability to make groups is an important skill in learning place value, the basis of our number system.

26. *A Handy Calculator*
What You Need:

Cardboard, marking pen, scissors

How to Make:

Make two cutouts of the child's hand. Number the fingers as shown. Ask him questions like those in "How Many More?" (Game 24, page 97), or "And Even More," (Game 25, above), and help him to solve them on his *Handy Calculator,* just as he did with his fingers or

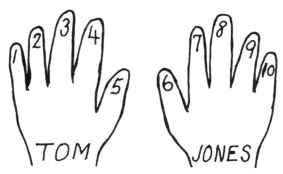

with pennies. Show him that he can place his own fingers directly on the corresponding fingers of the calculator and use the number symbols as well as counting procedures. Go slowly with this game.

27. *Card Sums*

This game is an extension of "Pairs of Cards" (Game 15, page 90). Besides making pairs, the players can build sums. For example, if there is a Two on the table, and a player has a Three and a Five in his hand, he says, "I am adding my Three to that Two to make five." He places all three cards on his pile. Then he takes two additional cards from the top of the unused portion of the deck to replace the two removed from his hand.

28. *Ready to Write*

Writing numbers is a difficult task, and requires several different skills.
What You Need:
Felt or sandpaper, ten 3 x 5-inch cards, glue, scissors, marking pen
How to Make:
Draw each number—0, 1, 2, 3, 4, 5, 6, 7, 8, 9—about 10 cm (4 in) high on felt. Cut them out, and glue each numeral to a different card. Mark the bottom of each card with a wavy line.

How to Play:

Ask your child to trace each number with his finger, then draw it in the air. He can match these numerals with those in his books, in ads, on the clock, and other places.

What Else Can You Do?

• Hand him a number card under the table. Ask him to trace it without looking, and tell you what number it is.

• He can shape pipecleaners into numerals.

29. *Number Shapes*

What You Need:

Play dough or cookie dough

How to Play:

Working on just a few numbers at a time, have your child shape the numerals. Cookie dough can be baked.

30. *Writing Numbers*

What You Need:

Red and black pens, paper

How to Play:

Make a dot outline of each numeral. Start with a red dot, and make the others black. Your child then follows the dots. When he is ready, he will write the numbers without guidance.

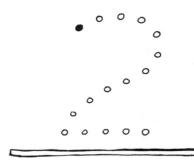

31. *Play Store*
    What You Need:
    Grocery cans and cartons, small cards, crayons, adhesive tape, money box, pennies and nickels
    How to Play:
    Suggest to your child that he be the storekeeper and you be the customer. He can arrange his stock on shelves, attaching to each item a price tag on which he has written the numbers he knows. Purchase the articles, using real pennies and nickels. Have him make change when necessary. This game uses many skills. Play it often.

32. *Counting On*
    What You Need:
    Ten pennies, *Handy Calculator* (Game 26, page 98)
    How to Play:
    Make two groups of pennies, with four in the first group and three in the second group. Ask your child how many pennies are in each group. How many altogether? Children usually start from "one" when they count to find the total number in two groups.
    Show your child how to "count on." Point to the first group: "How many here?...Yes, four." Point to each penny in the second group as you say: "Five, six, seven. There are seven pennies altogether."
    Make other combinations of pennies, and ask your child to count on to find the total number of pennies.
    Repeat the four-and-three combination of pennies. Then show your child how to count on with the *Handy Calculator*. Place a penny on each "finger" of the *Handy Calculator* so that she sees the relationship between the two problems. Then ask her to do the same problem with her own fingers, again using the "count on" procedure.
    Repeat the same problem, starting with a group of three then counting on: "Four, five, six, seven."

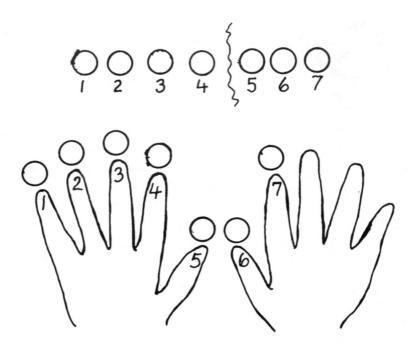

Eventually your child will learn the addition combinations.

What Else Can You Do?

• Show your child how to "count on" to make change. To give change from two nickels for an item costing seven cents, he counts: "Eight, nine, ten," as she gives the customer three cents in change. Role-play a game in which you make change.

• Another type of problem that can be solved by "counting on" goes like this: "I need seven cents to buy a cookie. I have only three cents. How many more pennies do I need?" Help your child to work it out with pennies, the *Handy Calculator,* and her fingers.

33. *Fractions*

What You Need:

Three apples; a knife

How to Play:

Cut one apple into two equal pieces, each called a "half." Put the two pieces together to form a "whole" apple, "one" apple.

Cut another apple into four equal "fourths" or "quarters." Show your child that four quarters form a whole apple, and two quarters form a half apple. Show her three-quarters of an apple.

Cut the last apple into thirds, and follow the same procedure.

What Else Can You Do?

• Look for other occasions to talk about fractions. For example, fold a sheet of paper in half and cut a design through the fold. Fold other sheets in quarters (two different ways) and cut the same pattern. Compare the sheets when they are open.

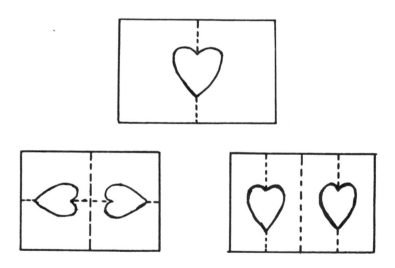

34. *Order Counts*

What You Need:

Five different small toys

How to Play:

Arrange the toys in a line.

"How many toys are there?...Yes, five toys. The truck is number one in the line. That means the truck is first. The ball is number two in the line; it is second." Continue to discuss the remaining toys the same way.

Then ask your child to arrange the toys in line in a different order, and repeat the whole procedure. Ask your child which is first, which is fourth, etc. In which position is the blue car? These numbers are called the ordinal numbers.

Counting can start at one end or at the other end of the line. Sometimes there is no choice, as when waiting at the checkout in the supermarket.

What Else Can You Do?

• Practice with more than five objects.

• Practice counting backwards: the fifth, the fourth, etc.

• Use ordinal numbers when you and your child are waiting in line. As customers check out, different people become first in line in the market.

• Use ordinal numbers when serving food to the members of the family, or discussing a line of parked cars.

35. *Egg Carton Pairs*
What You Need:

Egg carton, ten counters (beans, buttons, etc.)

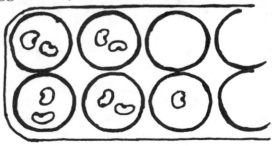

How to Play:

Pick up a handful of counters. Let your child count them and then tell you whether the number is odd or even. Pairs of things make even numbers. She can check by dropping two counters into each cup of the egg carton. If one is left over, the number is odd.

Can she count the beans in the egg carton by twos— 2, 4, 6, etc.? This is called "skip-counting."

36. *Odd and Even*
How to Play:

"Let's take turns counting. You say 'one,' I'll say 'two,' you say 'three,'" and so on. Explain that one, three, five, etc. are odd numbers, and two, four, six, etc. are even. Zero is also even. Look for odd and even house numbers, license plates, price tags.

37. *Fill the Egg Carton*
What You Need:

Egg carton, forty-eight beans, cards numbered 1 to 9
How to Play:

There are two players. Each one takes twenty-four beans. The rule is that each cup may hold four beans. Each player owns six cups on one side of the box. The game ends when one player fills all of her six cups.

Place the cards face down on the table. The first player chooses a card, say a Six. She picks up six of her beans, places four in the first cup on the left, and two in the next cup. Then the second player does the same. Shuffle the cards after each move.

At her second turn, the first player continues to fill the second cup until it has four beans, then proceeds to the third cup.

The game may also be played on a large sheet of paper which has been ruled like an egg carton with two

rows of six cups. This makes counting the beans an easier task.
What Else Can You Do?
  • Make the rule "two in each cup," or three, or five.
  • Use a six-sided die, instead of cards, to determine how many beans are to be used at each move.

38. *Counting Beyond Ten*
  A child must memorize the number words from zero to twelve. Larger numbers have a definite structure that is based on grouping by tens. Help your child to understand the structure. "Twenty" means "two tens," and "fifteen" means "five and ten." The word "fourteen" seems to be backwards when compared with "twenty-four," and this can be confusing to a child.
  Rhythmic counting helps children to remember the words. Your child can sing or chant "Band of Angels" (page 82) with the following word changes:
  Substitute "ten, twenty, thirty,..." for "one, two, three...."
  Substitute eleven to twenty for one to ten.
  Sing it twice through to count all twenty "digits" (fingers and toes) on hands and feet. In Spanish the word *dedo (dedos,* plural) names both finger and toe.
What Else Can You Do?
  • When several people are in the room, ask your child how many fingers are in the room. How many toes? How many fingers and toes together?

39. *Dimes and Pennies*
What You Need:
  Ten dimes, twenty pennies
How to Play:
  Explain that both one dime and ten pennies are called "ten cents." Ask your child to give you change for a dime, then for two dimes.

Show her three dimes and two pennies, and ask her to name the sum. Repeat with other sums. Then ask her to form a certain sum. Can she do it another way? Forming sums with dimes and pennies is good preparation for learning our place-value number system, which requires grouping by tens.

40. *Writing Two-digit Numbers*
What You Need:
Ten dimes, ten pennies, pencil, paper

Ten ¹⁰	One ¹
2	4

How to Play:
Tell the child "We are going to write how much money we have." Make a group of two dimes and four pennies. "How many dimes?...How many pennies?... I will write 2 in this column, and 4 in that column. This T stands for Ten; each dime is worth ten cents. This O stands for One; each penny is worth one cent.

"Now tell me how many cents I have here.... Twenty-four cents. This number is twenty-four." Point to the written number. "It means two tens and four ones. Twenty-four."

Repeat with many other sums of dimes and pennies. What Else Can You Do?

• Write a two-digit number. Ask the child to give you that much money in dimes and pennies. Take turns.

41. *Sums of Money*
    What You Need:
        Two dimes, twenty pennies, pencil, paper

1 0	1
1	3
	4
1	7

1 0	1
1	7
	4
2	1

How to Play:
    Give your child a dime and three pennies. "How much money did I give you?...Can you write that? Now I will give you more money." Give her four pennies. "Write that under the other number....That's fine. How much money have you altogether?...Right. I'll draw a line; that means we are adding these two numbers. Write 17 under the line.

    "Here is a new problem. You have seventeen cents. I will give you four cents more. Tell me how much money you have....Right, twenty-one cents. But all those coins are so heavy. Can you show me twenty-one cents that won't be so heavy? Use fewer coins. Yes, you can exchange ten pennies for a dime. Now write that problem on the paper."

    Making exchanges is basic in learning addition.

42. *Take Away Money*
    What You Need:
        Two dimes, twenty pennies, pencil, paper
    How to Play:
        Give the child one dime and five pennies.

        "Here is some money for you. How much is it?...Yes, fifteen cents. I'd like you to give me back three cents....Thank you. How much money have you

10	1
1	5
−	3
1	2

10	1
1	2
−	3
	9

now?...Please give me three more cents....Why can't you?...You have only two pennies? Can you do anything with that dime?...Yes, you can exchange the dime for ten pennies....How many pennies have you?...Yes, you have twelve pennies....Please give me three. How many have you now?" Help the child to write these transactions. Explain that the minus sign means "take away."

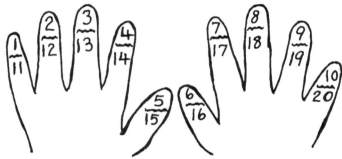

What Else Can You Do?

• Extend the *Handy Calculator* (Game 26, page 98) to twenty by adding two cutouts of your child's feet, with the toes numbered from eleven to twenty. Later you can write this second set of numbers on the fingers of the *Handy Calculator*. Help the child to do sums and differences with numbers up to twenty, both with the *Handy Calculator* and with her fingers.

• Some children like to work with a string of twenty large beads, with the colors alternating for every five beads.

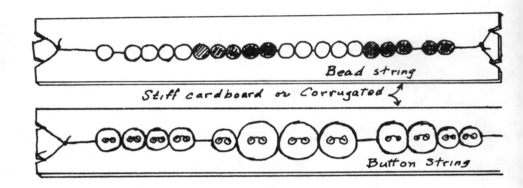

43. *Pennies, Nickels, Dimes*
What You Need:
    Ten nickels, ten dimes, twenty pennies, pencil, paper
How to Play:
    This game involves many different skills.
    Skip-counting: Give your child three nickels, and ask how much money she has. Encourage her to count by fives. Do the same with dimes and counting by tens.
    Exchanging: Give her a dime, two nickels, and three pennies. Ask her how much money she has. Can she show the same amount using fewer coins? Ask her to do addition and subtraction problems with the coins, as in the two preceding games. Name an amount, and ask her to represent it in money in more than one way.
    Writing: Ask her to write her transactions.
    Play store or restaurant to give her the opportunity to use all these skills.

44. *What Comes?*
How to Play:
    Establish one of two rules: either "what comes before" or "what comes after." One person names a number and the other names the number that comes

before or after. Take turns. Play this game at any odd moment.

45. *Follow the Rule*
    This game develops skill in mental arithmetic.

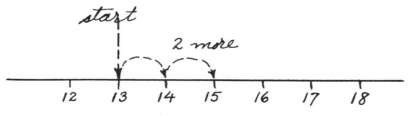

How to Play:
    Establish a rule, like "two more than." One person names a number and the other names the number that is two more than the first number. The second person then either repeats the second number, or names an entirely different number.
    Some children find that a measuring tape or number line (help the child to make one, as illustrated) is helpful at first.

46. *Guess My Number*
    How to Play:
    Ask your child to write a number on a piece of paper, and hide it. Then ask questions that she can answer with yes or no: "Is it even?" "Is it between 15 and 30?"

47. *Break the Bank*
    Several people can play at the same time. This is a good game for practicing place value and exchange.
    What You Need:
    Ten dimes and ten pennies for each player (real or play money), one dollar, paper, pencil, two bowls, and a six-sided die.

100	10	1
	o	OO
	o	OO
	o	O
		O
		O

How to Make:

Each player needs a chart with headings as shown.

How to Play:

Place all the money—the dimes in one bowl, the pennies in another—in the center of the table. This is the bank.

Each player takes a turn tossing the die to determine how many pennies she may collect from the bank. When a player has ten pennies, she may exchange them for one dime. The first player to trade for the dollar is the winner.

What Else Can You Do?

• Use two dice instead of one, to make the game go faster.

• Play with pennies, nickels, and quarters, grouping by fives. A nickel equals five pennies, and a quarter equals five nickels. Head the charts: 25—5—1

• Use two kinds of counters instead of coins. The headings on the chart can be 4, 2, 1; or 9, 3, 1; or 16, 4, 1; etc.

• Play in reverse: Start with 100 pennies, and deposit money in the bank.

48. *Mathematical Symbols*

The use of mathematical symbols in the early grades causes difficulty for many children. Here are several ways you can make it easier to learn:

Read the symbols in everyday language.

Apply the symbols to real objects and situations.

Ask the child to make up a story about the mathematical sentence.

Examples:

$3 + 2 = \square$ How many are three and two? Joan had three trucks. Her father gave her two more trucks. How many trucks did she have?

$3 + \square = 5$ Three and what number make five? I have three cents. How many more cents will I need so that I will have five cents?

$5 > 3$ Five is more than three. Five is a bigger number than three. Five cookies are more than three cookies.

$3 < 5$ Three is less than five. Three is a smaller number than five. Three apples are fewer than five apples.

49. *Bowl Game*

This Native American game gives children experience with the laws of chance and keeping score. Several can play.

What You Need:

Four peach or plum pits, small bowl, marking pen, about sixty toothpicks

How to Make:

Draw a band on one side of each pit.

How to Play:

The first player places all the pits into the bowl, and dumps them on the ground. How many pits have the marked side up? She takes a toothpick for each marked pit.

The second player does the same, then the third, etc. Each player has ten turns. At the end of the game, the player with the most toothpicks is the winner.

The toothpicks can be arranged 卌 for ease in counting by fives.

What Else Can You Do?

• Mark each pit with a different number of bands, and assign a different number of points to each.

50. *Dreidl Game*

During Hanukkah, the Jewish Festival of Lights, which occurs in December, children love to spin the dreidl, a four-sided top. They celebrate the miracle that occurred over 2,000 years ago when the Maccabees recaptured the temple of Jerusalem. Although there was hardly enough oil to keep the lamps burning just one night, somehow it lasted for eight days.

On each side of the dreidl is inscribed a letter, spelling the initials of the message "A great miracle happened there," or *G, M, H, T,* in English. This game gives children experience with the laws of chance and keeping score. Several can play.

What You Need:

8-cm (3-in) cardboard square; thin dowel rod or lollipop stick; pencil; paper

How to Make:

Print the letters *G, M, H,* and *T* along the sides of the square. Draw the diagonals to locate the center of the square, and push the stick through it.

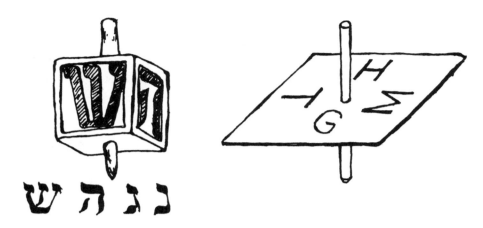

ש ה ג נ

How to Play:

Spin the dreidl twenty times. Record how many times each letter is uppermost as it falls.

Before each spin ask your child to guess which letter will be up. Is there any way of predicting?

To make the game competitive, assign a different number of points to each letter on the *dreidl.*

G	卌 ‖	7
M	‖‖‖	4
H	‖‖	3
T	卌 ‖	6
		20

51. *Guesstimation*

Children enjoy big numbers. Challenge your child to work out ways of "guesstimating" such quantities as the number of kernels on an ear of corn; the number of leaves on a bush, branch, or tree; the number of beans in a jar. A child can count the number of kernels in one row of corn and multiply by the number of rows. She can spread the beans on a checkerboard, count the number covering one square, and multiply by the number of squares the beans cover. What strategies can she devise on her own?

52. *Get Ready for Wari*

Games 52, 53, and 54 introduce Wari. This African game, also played in versions known by such names as Oware, Ayo, Kalah, Mancala, and many others, helps to promote friendly relations among peoples. Considered one of the world's best mathematical games, it can be played by champions as well as by first graders. The rules are simple; the strategies can be complex.
What You Need:

Two-row egg carton, ten large beans

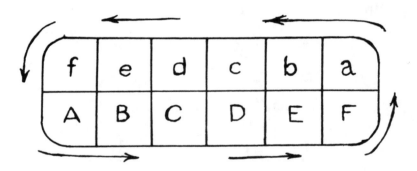

How to Play:

Ask your child to pick up a handful of beans and count them. She places the handful in any cup of the egg carton.

Suppose she places them in cup B. "In this game you will pick up all the beans in that cup (B) and drop one bean in each of these cups, going all around the egg carton." Point to cups C, D, etc. as you talk. "Before you do that, can you tell me where the last bean will fall?"

She checks her answer by actually dropping the beans into the cups. Take turns doing this.

53. *Easy Wari*
What You Need:
Egg carton cut down to two rows of four cups, sixteen large beans (or other counters), two small bowls for storing captured beans

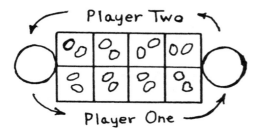

Player Two

Player One

Player One's first move

How to Play:
There are two players. Each has four cups on one side of the "board," and each has a storage bowl ("endpot") on her right. To start: Place two beans in each cup.

Moves: Player One picks up all the beans in one of her cups, and drops one in each cup going around the board to the right.

Player Two makes a similar move, starting on his side of the board. The players alternate turns.

Capture: If the last bean in any move makes a group of two in a cup on the opponent's side, these beans are captured and placed in the player's endpot. Also, if the cups just preceding this last cup (on the opponent's side) contain two beans, these beans may be captured.

Finish: The game ends when one person has no beans on her side. Play for fun, not to win.

Player One is ready
to move

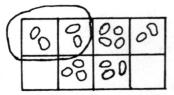

Player One has moved

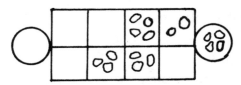

Player One has captured 4 beans

Let your child test several different moves in order
to develop strategy. Set up a "capture" situation, as
shown, and let your child work out ways of handling it.

54. *The Real Wari Game*
What You Need:
Egg carton with two rows of six cups, forty-eight
beans, two storage bowls
How to Play:
The rules are the same as for Easy Wari (Game 53,
p. 117), with these differences:
Start: Place four beans in each of the twelve cups.
Capture: When the last bean makes a group of two
or three in the opponent's cup, and in the preceding
cups.
Finish: When one player has no beans left on her
side, the opponent must move so that this player is
given some beans, if at all possible. When one or two
beans remain on the board, they go to the player whose
side they are on. The winner is the person who has
captured the most beans.
What Else Can You Do?
• Divide the board among three or four players.
• Encourage your child to invent other rules.

Appendices

A.

The Metric System

Length: Meter (m)—approximately 40 inches (a foot is about 30 centimeters; a centimeter is 0.4 of an inch)
Capacity: Liter (l)—slightly more than one quart
Weight (mass): Kilogram (kg)—about 2.2 pounds

METRIC PREFIXES

*Centi*meter (cm)—0.01 meter (1/100 meter)
*Milli*meter (mm)—0.001 meter (1/1000 meter)
*Kilo*meter (km)—1000 meters

B.

Recommended Children's Books

The best source is Sharon Young's *Mathematics in Children's Books* (see Appendix G, p. 134).

The books listed here either are not included in Young's book, or are unusual in some way.

Anno, Mitsumasa. *Anno's Counting Book.* New York: T. Y. Crowell, 1977. Exquisite picture book about the twelve months of the year.

Carle, Eric. The author has written several books for very young children.

Feelings, Muriel and Tom. *Moja Means One: The Swahili Counting Book.* New York: Dial, 1971; Pied Piper, 1976 (paperback). Numbers 1 to 10, with beautiful scenes of Africa.

Hoban, Tana. Ms. Hoban is the author of many books of photographs illustrating geometric and other concepts for the very young.

Wahl, John and Stacey. *I Can Count the Petals of a Flower.* National Council of Teachers of Mathematics, 1976. Color photographs of flowers illustrate numbers 1 to 16.

Walter, Marion. *Another, Another, Another and More.* London: André Deutsch, Ltd. Children explore with two hinged mirrors (included).

———. *Look at Annette.* New York: Evans, 1972; distributed by Dutton. Paperback title: *Another Magic*

Mirror Book. Scholastic. Great fun with a mirror (included).

_____. *Make a Bigger Puddle, Make a Smaller Worm*. New York: Evans, 1972; distributed by Dutton. Paperback title: *The Magic Mirror Book*. Scholastic. Mirror is included.

Zaslavsky, Claudia. *Count on Your Fingers African Style*. New York: T. Y. Crowell, 1980. Picture book shows finger counting in African cultures and our own.

C.

Songs and Singing Games

Songs About Numbers. Folk songs are my favorites. many are included in the three collections listed below, keyed by number to the songs. FC denotes Folkways record.

(1) Landeck, Beatrice. *Songs to Grow On.* New York: Marks Music Corp., 1950.
(2) ———. *More Songs to Grow On.* New York: Marks Music Corp., 1954.
(3) Seeger, Ruth Crawford. *American Folk Songs for Children.* New York: Doubleday, 1948.

(All three books are available from the Children's Book and Music Center.)

(1) "Band of Angels." Numbers one to ten. (FC 7624)
(1, 3) "By'm By." Numbers one to nine. (FC 7020, FC 7624)
"Children Go Where I Send Thee." Numbers one to ten. (FC 7624)
(2) "Ha, Ha, This-A-Way." For any birthday. (FC 7526)
(2) "New River Train." One to ten. (FC 7674)
(1) "The Story of Twelve." From twelve to one.
"Ten Green Bottles." From ten to one. (FC 7662)
(1, 3) "This Old Man." One to ten. (FC 7545, FC 7601, FC 7625, FC 7637)

(2) "Three Craw." First to fourth.
   "The Twelve Days of Christmas." First to twelfth.
(3) "Who Built the Ark? Noah, Noah." Two to ten.

Singing Games for spatial concepts.

Did You Ever See a Lassie?
Go In and Out the Window.
Hokey Pokey (change "left" and "right" to "one" and "the other")
London Bridge
Looby Loo
Ring Around a Rosie

D.

Beautiful Junk

Bottle caps, jar lids
Boxes, containers with lids, cans
Cards, envelopes, paper
Dowel rods
Egg and milk cartons
Magazines with colored pictures
Patterned cloth, wallpaper samples, wrapping paper
Pebbles and shells
Plastic cups, plates, spoons, drinking straws, bowls
Popsicle sticks and tongue depressors
String and ribbons
Styrofoam trays and packaging materials
Toothpicks
Tubes from toilet tissue and paper towels
Washers

E.

Commercial Materials

** Most important
* Desirable
# For school-age children

  Abacus #
  Attribute blocks (like *Shapes* in Chapter 4)
 *Beads (large)
**Blocks
 *Calculator # (four functions, liquid crystal display)
 *Cubes
  Cuisenaire rods
  Dice
  Geoboards
  Grid paper #
 *Kaleidoscope
 *Linking cubes or Unifix cubes
  Magnetic numerals (use them on the refrigerator!)
 *Measuring tape #
 *Mirrors
  Pegboard
 *Rulers #
 *Scissors
  Thermometer #

F.

Board and Table Games

Bingo and Lotto
Cards
Checkers
Chinese checkers
Connect the Dots
Dominoes (like *Two-squares,* Chapter 6)
Jigsaw puzzles
Mazes
Morris games (three-in-a-row)
Origami
Tangrams
Tic-tac-toe
Wari (Mancala, Kalah, Oware, Ayo)

G.

Adult Books and Resources

Arnold, Arnold. *The World Book of Children's Games.* Crowell, 1972. Games of strategy and many others.

Ginsburg, Herbert. *Children's Arithmetic.* Van Nostrand, 1977 (paperback). Children's strategies with arithmetic and the sources of their mistakes are explored by this psychologist.

Golick, Margie. *Deal Me In! The Use of Playing Cards in Learning and Teaching.* Norton, 1973. Over a hundred games, diversions, and tricks for children aged four and up, classified by age level.

Grunfeld, Frederick V., ed. *Games of the World.* Ballantine, 1975 (paperback). Over a hundred games, beautiful illustrations.

Holt, Michael and Zoltan P. Dienes. *Let's Play Math.* Walker, 1973. Puzzles and games of logic for age four and up.

Kohl, Herbert R. *Math, Writing, and Games.* N.Y. Review of Books, distributed by Vintage Books, 1974 (paperback). How to adapt standard games to the level of young children, how to play noncompetitively, and how to invent new games.

Lorton, Mary Baratta. *Mathematics Their Way,* 1976.

———. *Workjobs: Activity-Centered Learning for Early Childhood Education.* 1972.

_____. *Workjobs...for Parents: Activity-Centered Learning in the Home.* 1975. Addison-Wesley. Beautiful photographs illustrate all the activities.

Parents' Choice. A review of children's media. Box 185, Waban, Massachusetts 02168. Six issues per year.

Simons, Robin. *Recyclopedia: Games, Science Equipment, and Crafts from Recycled Materials.* Houghton Mifflin, 1976. Developed at the Boston Children's Museum.

Young, Sharon. *Mathematics in Children's Books: An Annotated Bibliography, Preschool Through Grade 3.* Creative Publications, 1979 (paperback, $2.25). Over 400 books listed according to math topic.

H.

Resource Catalogs

Send for their catalogs, free of charge except where noted.

Addison-Wesley Publishing Company
    South Street
    Reading, Massachusetts 01867
    Request brochures of Mary Baretta-Lorton's books.

Childcraft Education Corp.
    20 Kilmer Road
    Edison, New Jersey 08817
    The Growing Years Catalog

Children's Book and Music Center
    5373 West Pico Boulevard
    Los Angeles, California 90019
    Send one dollar for their fine list of children's books
    and records, as well as books and resources for adults.

Creative Publications
    P.O. Box 10328
    Palo Alto, California 94303
    Exclusively mathematics; books and materials for
    children, adult books and resources.

T.Y. Crowell Company—Dept. 363
    10 East 53rd Street

New York, N.Y. 10022
Write for *Mathematics Books for Curriculum Enrichment*

Cuisenaire Company of America, Inc.
12 Church Street
New Rochelle, N.Y. 10805
Exclusively mathematics; books and materials for children, adult books and resources.

Folkways Records and Service Corporation
43 West 62nd Street
New York, N.Y. 10023
Catalog of recordings for children.

National Association for the Education of Young Children
1834 Connecticut Avenue, N.W.
Washington, D.C. 20009
Catalog of publications.

Scholastic Book Services
904 Sylvan Avenue
Englewood Cliffs, N.J. 07632
Reader's Choice, catalog of inexpensive paperback books.

The Supply Room
P.O. Box 96
Great Neck, N.Y. 11022
Distributor for Milton Bradley, Playskool, Ideal.

Index

Age level, 9

Chance, games of, 113–15
Comparing, concepts of
  games 9, 20, 22–26, 27–29, 52, 64
  vocabulary, 20
Conversation, importance of. *See* Learning of
  language
Counting
  zero, 37, 83–86
  one to three, 30–37, 83–86
  four, 37, 83–86
  five, 86–92
  six to nine, 87–88, 92
  ten, 92–93
  ten to a hundred, 106–10
  See also Number concepts
Counting, types of
  finger, 92–93, 94, 96–97, 98–99, 101–02, 109
  rote, 3, 31–32, 82–83, 106
  skip, 105, 110–11
  use in measuring, 61, 65–68, 71–80
Cultures
  African, 43–45, 59, 116–18
  Chinese, 53–54
  holidays, 57
  Japanese, 57
  Jewish, 114–15
  Native American, 113–14
  of parents, 10–11

Estimation, 61, 65–66, 67–69, 73–76, 81, 115–17

Game preparation, 9–12
Graphing, 76

Learning
  capacity for, xi
  evaluation of, 4–5, 6–7
  of language, xi-xii, 1, 3–5, 6, 10, 12, 13, 20, 30
  of number concepts, 30, 81
  parental role in, 1–7, 12
  stages in, 1–3

Mapping, 58
Materials used in games, 10, 11–12
Mathematical symbols, 112–13
  See also Numerals
Mathematics
  ability to learn, xii
  need for, xi
  in school curriculum, xi
Measurement concepts
  experiences with, 61
  games for developing skills in, 9, 65–80
  See also Comparing: Measurements; Ordering
Measurements
  of capacity, 27–28, 61, 63, 68–71, 74–75, 79–80
  in informal units, 61, 71–78
  linear, 22–26, 29, 52, 61–64, 65–66, 67–68, 71–73, 75–77, 79
  in standard units, 61, 73, 79–80
  of temperature, 79
  of time, 61, 66–67, 78
  of weight (mass), 20, 28–29, 61, 64, 73–74, 77–78, 79–80
  See also Measurement concepts
Mental arithmetic, 110–11
Metric system, 10, 61, 79–80
Mirrors, games with, 41, 56
Money, games with, 96–99, 101–02, 106–10, 111–12

Number concepts
  fractions, 102–03
  games for developing skills in, 9–10, 30–37, 82–118
  odd and even numbers, 104–05

ordinal numbers, 103-04
skills required to learn, 3, 30, 81
two-digit numbers, 107-10
vocabulary, 30
See also Counting
Numerals
recognition of, 92, 94-96, 105-06
writing, 99-101, 107-10
Numerical operations
addition, 33-34, 37, 86, 87-88, 93, 97-99, 101-02, 108, 110-11
counting on, 101-02, 109-10
exchange, 97-98, 106-10, 111-12
grouping, 96-98, 105-10, 113-15, 117-18
multiplication, 115-16
one-to-one, 35, 37, 86, 90-91, 93
subtraction, 36-37, 85, 86, 108-10

Ordering, concepts of, 29, 61-64, 65, 103-04
See also Measurement concepts; Measurements

Paper, games with, 54-59
Patterns, 39-41, 47, 51-52, 53-54, 55-58, 59

Scoring, 113-15
Shape concepts
experiences with, 13, 39
games for developing skills in, 9, 15-19, 40-41, 42-43, 45-54, 59
vocabulary, 13
Shapes games, 45-54, 89-92
Sorting, concepts of
experiences with, 20
games for developing skills in, 9, 20-22, 26-27, 48, 49, 89-90
vocabulary, 20
Spatial concepts
experiences with, 13, 39
games for developing skills in, 9, 13-15, 19, 39-42, 43-45, 54-59
vocabulary, 13
Strategy, games of, 43-45, 116-18